T0328759

Cambridge Elements ≡

Elements in Shakespeare and Pedagogy
edited by
Liam E. Semler
University of Sydney
Gillian Woods
Birkbeck College, University of London

SHAKESPEARE AND VIRTUAL REALITY

Edited by

Stephen Wittek
Carnegie Mellon University

David McInnis
University of Melbourne

CAMBRIDGE
UNIVERSITY PRESS

CAMBRIDGE
UNIVERSITY PRESS

University Printing House, Cambridge CB2 8BS, United Kingdom

One Liberty Plaza, 20th Floor, New York, NY 10006, USA

477 Williamstown Road, Port Melbourne, VIC 3207, Australia

314–321, 3rd Floor, Plot 3, Splendor Forum, Jasola District Centre,
New Delhi – 110025, India

103 Penang Road, #05–06/07, Visioncrest Commercial, Singapore 238467

Cambridge University Press is part of the University of Cambridge.

It furthers the University's mission by disseminating knowledge in the pursuit of
education, learning, and research at the highest international levels of excellence.

www.cambridge.org
Information on this title: www.cambridge.org/9781009001878
DOI: 10.1017/9781009003995

First published 2021

A catalogue record for this publication is available from the British Library.

ISBN 978-1-009-00187-8 Paperback
ISSN 2632-816X (online)
ISSN 2632-8151 (print)

Additional resources for this publication at www.cambridge.org/wittek-mcinnis

Shakespeare and Virtual Reality

Elements in Shakespeare and Pedagogy

DOI: 10.1017/9781009003995

First published online: December 2021

Stephen Wittek
Carnegie Mellon University

David McInnis
University of Melbourne

Author for correspondence: Stephen Wittek, swittek@andrew.cmu.edu

ABSTRACT: Teaching Shakespeare through performance has a long history, and active methods of teaching and learning are a logical complement to the teaching of performance. Virtual reality ought to be the logical extension of such active learning, providing an unrivalled immersive experience of performance that overcomes historical and geographical boundaries. But what are the key advantages and disadvantages of virtual reality, especially as it pertains to Shakespeare? And, more interesting, what can Shakespeare do for virtual reality (rather than vice versa)? This Element, the first on its topic, explores the ways that virtual reality can be used in the classroom and the ways that it might radically change how students experience and think about Shakespeare in performance.

This Element also has a video abstract:
www.cambridge.org/shakespeare-and-vr

KEYWORDS: Shakespeare, virtual reality, digital humanities, theatre, pedagogy

ISBNs: 9781009001878 (PB), 9781009003995 (OC)

ISSNs: 2632-816X (online), 2632-8151 (print)

Contents

Contributors

Emily Bryan
Sacred Heart University

Justin Carpenter
Independent Scholar

Scott Hollifield
University of Nevada Las Vegas

Jennifer A. Low
Florida Atlantic University

David McInnis
University of Melbourne

Jennifer Roberts-Smith
University of Waterloo

Erin Sullivan
Shakespeare Institute, University of Birmingham

Michael Ullyot
University of Calgary

Stephen Wittek
Carnegie Mellon University

Introduction

Stephen Wittek
David McInnis

Following the arrival of affordable, mass-market headsets and an ever-growing body of producers and consumers, it is now clear that virtual reality (VR) is here to stay for the foreseeable future. Alongside gaming and entertainment, one of the main industries helping to usher the new medium into the mainstream has been education, with institutions making investments in various VR-related technologies and researchers developing media for everything from language instruction to surgical training and flight simulation. In the humanities, a key locus of virtual reality development has been Shakespeare studies, which over the past few years has seen the emergence of VR-centred research endeavours such as the *Shakespeare-VR* Project (see Section 8) and innovative, full-length VR productions, such as *Hamlet 360* (see Section 6). At first glance, intersections along these lines seem inevitable given the ubiquity of Shakespearean drama in the academy, high school curricula, and multiple cultures worldwide. Indeed, since the early twentieth century, the introduction of new media technology – film, radio, television, video, the Internet – has found producers turning to Shakespeare as a source for content and cultural prestige, and educators enthusiastically embracing new means of presenting Shakespearean drama to students. On a similar note, the immersive capabilities of virtual reality seem tailor-made for the long-established practice of teaching Shakespeare through 'active learning', a pedagogical approach that gets students out of their seats, acting and vocalising, in order to emphasise the interpretive utility of space, embodiment, and movement. In short, if it is now clear that virtual reality is here to stay, it is also clear that Shakespeare will have a prominent presence in the virtual multiverse.

In this brief Element, we have brought together a diverse group of Shakespeare scholars, digital humanists, theatrical producers, media theorists, and pedagogical researchers to explore the intersection between Shakespeare and virtual reality, especially as it pertains to education. For the most part, our use of the term 'virtual reality' refers to the experience furnished by a head-mounted display that immerses users in a simulated world. However, we have also made an effort to address other technologies and experiences regularly described as 'virtual', including augmented reality (the overlay of virtual objects onto the real world) (see Section 4), and the 'virtual classroom' convened by telecommunications technologies such as Zoom (see Section 5).

We begin, in Part I, by asking the most basic question of all – why Shakespeare and virtual reality? – and identify the key issues and ideas that define the topic. For Jennifer Roberts-Smith, whose scholarly work combines theatrical practice with virtual reality production, the pathway to substantive engagement with the medium begins by considering what Shakespeare can do for VR, rather than vice versa (Section 1). In an assessment that cuts through the hyperbole surrounding the rush to embrace virtual technologies, she develops a clear-eyed account of what virtual experience is and is not, and offers some suggestions for how to make virtual reality more Shakespearean, not merely in terms of content, but also in terms of artistic rigour and affective resonance. In the following section, Scott Hollifield expands on Roberts-Smith's argument by pointing towards affinities between virtuality and Shakespeare's dramatic technique, and by bringing the advent of Shakespeare and virtual reality into connection with the history and theory of Shakespeare on film. Together, the sections in Part I enable teachers and students to better explore the influence of Shakespeare on new media forms and reconsider how studying the experimental and multimedia theatre of Shakespeare's day better prepares us for engaging with new technologies in our own time.

Having situated the development of VR in its historical and intellectual context relative to Shakespeare studies in Part I, Part II proceeds to consider specific case studies by David McInnis (Section 3) and Emily Bryan (Section 4) that offer detailed first-hand accounts of experiments with virtual reality, augmented reality, and related technologies in connection to Shakespeare pedagogy. Erin Sullivan then ventures further into pedagogical theory, assessing the biases inherent in concepts of the virtual, and considering how such biases impact classroom dynamics (Section 5). Besides exploring the consumption and production of immersive media in classrooms, each of these sections addresses urgent equity issues, in particular the socio-economic and physical considerations around the use of technology. In 2021, representative retail prices start at as little as US $10 for Google Cardboard headsets that work with smartphones to enable users to have virtual reality experiences, but contrary to popular presumptions, not all students have access to such headsets, smartphones, or sufficiently fast Wi-Fi to guarantee that teaching with VR is an efficient experience. Those students who do have access to the right tools may still be excluded from participation by physical hurdles (motion sickness, monocular vision, etc.), normative assumptions about gender, or a lack of digital literacy (age is no guarantor of technological fluency). An implicit question throughout this section, then, concerns the extent to which we can make VR a more inclusive technology.

Moving from the classroom to productions, Part III begins with Michael Ullyot's critical overview (Section 6) of some of the most notable VR adaptations of Shakespeare from the past few years, offering provocations for how future developers of VR technology might learn from successful stagings of Shakespeare's plays (thus speaking to Jennifer Roberts-Smith's concerns in Section 1); it will be of immediate interest to anyone teaching Shakespeare in performance. Turning the model of adaptation in these productions on its head, Jennifer A. Low (Section 7) analyses Red Bull Theater's 2019 presentation of John Webster's *The White Devil*, a production that used VR headsets as props, thereby putting Jacobean revenge tragedy in dialogue with present-day discourse around the virtual. Low's section provides a witty, metatheatrical answer-of-sorts to Jennifer Roberts-Smith's challenge to think in terms of 'what Shakespeare can do for VR', expanding 'Shakespearean' to encompass the stage, stagecraft, and technologies of early modern theatre, and in particular the affordances available to Shakespeare's contemporary, Webster, whose *White Devil* was written circa 1611–12 and probably premiered at the original Red Bull playhouse in Clerkenwell, London. Finally, to draw further lines of connection between virtual reality, performance theory, and pedagogy, Stephen Wittek shares a candid account of his education project, *Shakespeare-VR*, tracing the project's course of development from inception to planning, filming, dissemination, and classroom testing (Section 8). Justin Carpenter's annotated bibliography will be invaluable to anyone commencing work on this topic.

I Why Shakespeare and Virtual Reality?

1 What Can Shakespeare Do for Virtual Reality?
Jennifer Roberts-Smith

Each new medium in which the works of William Shakespeare have been articulated and adapted has contributed to the expansion of 'Shakespeare' as a conceptual field. 'Shakespeare' is ever increasingly more than the formal aesthetic configurations that were possible in the early modern media in which Shakespeare's works were initially expressed (the stage and print drama). As the cumulative contributions of artists, audiences, scholars, educators, and students have demonstrated over the past four and a half centuries, 'Shakespeare' now constitutes an infinitude of potential forms, awaiting articulation in unknowable future media. 'Shakespeare' has meant what each successive community of makers and audiences has made of it, and will mean what each new community articulates in new media as they emerge.

No individual medium could have made its contribution to 'Shakespeare' unless we – all of us, as communities of makers and audiences – had conceived of 'Shakespeare' as more expansive than the affordances of any one medium in particular. As Shakespeare educators encountering virtual reality (VR) for the first time, we know from long experience with other media that VR is no more likely to have a medium-specific power to manifest or teach 'Shakespeare' more faithfully or more effectively – to clarify or expand 'Shakespeare' as a conceptual field – than any other new medium before it. 'Shakespeare' is not medium-specific; it is arguably essentially intermedial, both in its complex performative-textual origins and in its later multimedial manifestations. 'Shakespeare' enables the kinds of 'intersections and the spaces in-between the intersections' (Chapple and Kattenbelt 2006: 24) among media that constitute communicative spaces within which experience can occur and meaning can be derived (Boenisch 2006). New technologies do not bring new affordances to Shakespeare; rather, 'Shakespeare' (as that conceptual field has been understood and instantiated by artists, audiences, scholars, teachers, and students) will bring new opportunities for meaning-making to VR, just as it has to earlier technologies as they have emerged and have been configured in relation to one another.

Nevertheless, this is a beguiling moment in the emergence of VR as a medium, when the temptations of technological monomania, utopianism, and determinism are particularly acute. We have seen the 360-degree documentary film masterpiece *Clouds over Sidra* (Arora and Milk 2015) raise more than $3.8 billion in relief for Syrian refugees (Badsa 2017); we have read that 3D graphical simulations in the training of surgeons at the University of California, Los Angeles increased their success by 230 per cent (Blumstein 2019); and we acknowledge, along with the director of Commonwealth Shakespeare Company's *Hamlet 360*, that 'many young people's first experience of Shakespeare is not all that great' (Maler, cited in Harris 2019). Why wouldn't VR be just the thing to 'bring the material to life' for one and for all (Maler, cited in Harris 2019)? What follows here is a preliminary list of three propositions that might help to ground us as Shakespeare educators as we navigate the affordances that make VR seem so attractive. They are offered as a reminder that Shakespeare has at least as much to offer VR as VR does to Shakespeare. Virtual reality is one medium that can be leveraged in the open aesthetic system of 'Shakespeare', through which we engage our students in the processes of shared meaning-making that already animate our pedagogy.

Proposition 1: Like Shakespeare, VR is an open system. Rather than 'immersing' a participant in a hermetic illusion, VR highlights and generates meaning from the disjunctions between the virtual illusion and the participant's irreproducible, contingent sense of their own body and surroundings.

Virtual reality reconfigures the embodied relationship between spectator and screen by placing a participant at the centre of a spherical image that excludes other visual, auditory, tactile, and proprioceptive stimuli to varying degrees. Since VR's inception, VR hardware developers have conceptualised the technology as a system that aims to 'submerge the perceptual system of the participant in computer-generated stimuli' (Biocca and Delaney 1995). As a result of this governing concept, there is a general understanding that VR headsets are more immersive than, say, desktop computer screens, because they exclude the perception of visual stimuli not part of the virtual illusion (Dalgarno and Lee 2010: 11).

However, recent work in hardware design and software development has demonstrated that perceptual submersion does not hinge on the degree to which a VR system *excludes* sensory stimuli, but on the degree to which it *includes* stimuli participants expect to encounter in the real world. The most important factors are as follows:

- *Representational fidelity* – the degree to which a virtual illusion looks or sounds like reality.[1]
- *Interactivity* – the degree to which the illusion responds realistically to the embodied actions of a spectator.[2]
- *Identity construction* – the degree to which spectators can associate themselves with characters in the virtual environment.[3]

To date, VR developers have struggled to include enough sensory stimuli to make any given experience convincingly 'immersive'. A key challenge is the often-noted tendency of the technology to cause motion sickness in some participants, which derives from the disjunction between convincingly 'real' visual stimuli and less convincing tactile and proprioceptive stimuli.[4] Ironically, then, by aiming to completely overwhelm the participant's sensory perceptions, VR draws heightened attention to the senses it fails to overwhelm. The participant's body thus becomes a central signifier in any VR experience's aesthetic system, as is the case for spectators in the theatre. Ultimately, the system is open to all of the contingencies of sense, place, and preconception that participants bring with them.

New, aesthetically oriented work in virtual reality is beginning to explore the expressive potential of this salience of the body. For example, Paul Cegys and Joris Weijdom describe *The Blue Hour VR* (commissioned as part of the 2019 Prague Quadrennial's exploration of XR scenography, 36Q°) as 'explicitly focus[ing] on the interweave between different modes of sensing within the experiencer's physical body through the blending of real and virtual

---

[1]   See Bulu 2012; Dalgarno and Lee 2010; Fowler 2015; Kwon et al. 2012; Sanchez-Vives and Slater 2005.

[2]   See Dalgarno and Lee 2010; Kwon et al. 2012.

[3]   See Biocca, Harms, and Burgoon 2003; Bulu 2012; Fowler 2015.

[4]   See Weech, Kenny, and Barnett-Cowan 2019.

environments. This radically (re)position[s] the body of the experiencer at the locus of performance' (Cegys 2020). This understanding of embodiment in VR as the embodied experience of the participant in counterpoint to the virtual image significantly extends the usual understanding of VR embodiment as the identification of participants with elements of the virtual world, as part of the process of *identity construction*.[5] If we conceive of VR experiences as situated in each individual participant's body and incorporating the unique and unpredictable contingencies that each individual brings with them, we will necessarily acknowledge and encourage a much broader range of perceptions than a hermetically 'immersive' system can accommodate. In addition to enriching opportunities for meaning-making, this approach also opens new possibilities for representation in virtual worlds, which need no longer be tied to realism.

Proposition 2: Like Shakespeare, VR is intermedial. Rather than taking monomedial realism as its primary representational mode, it engages multiple media in stylistic impressionism, opening opportunities for interpretive agency.

Simulation of actual-world phenomena remains the design objective of most VR applications, using *either* 360-degree video (which is two-dimensional) *or* 3D graphics (which are also two-dimensional, but create an illusion of three-dimensionality). Shakespeare studies has largely focused on the documentation and/or simulation of live performance, most often using 360-degree video (Wittek's *Shakespeare-VR*; Maler's *Hamlet 360*), with some outliers exploring 3D-graphical renderings (Gochfield and Molina's *To Be with Hamlet*). As in most commercial applications, few attempts have been made to combine the two sub-media, because the aesthetic contrast between two and three dimensions has not generally been understood to be desirable. But if the stylistic contrast between 2D and 3D renderings were understood as a productive form of intermediality – one that deliberately leaves open 'the spaces in-between the intersections' between media (Chapple and Kattenbelt 2006: 24) in an intentionally impressionist aesthetic – we might leverage the ways those gaps can draw

[5] See, for example, Waterworth and Waterworth's (2014) 'distributed embodiment'.

attention to the perspectives that the work and the viewer are both taking, or might take differently, on the objects of their gaze.

In other aesthetic contexts, intermediality has been embraced as a means of generating interpretive experiences that might lead to more just social and environmental outcomes. One important example is the *imagineNative 2167 VR* touring exhibition (2018–19) which used impressionist scenography to reorient audiences' understanding of Indigeneity in Canada away from the dominant tendency to historicise a lost Indigenous past and towards Indigenous Futurism (www.tiff.net/the-review/indigenous-existence-is-resistance).[6] In each of the exhibition's four individual works, incongruencies among the subsidiary media employed disrupted VR's tendency to mono-medial simulation. For example, Kent Monkman's *Honour Dance* manifested the dances of the ritual figure 'Berdashe' in four directions simultaneously, and Scott Benesiinaabandan's *Blueberry Pie under a Martian Sky* floated participants through a cosmological space defined by abstract, three-dimensional geometric forms.[7]

Crucially, in intermedial works like these, the site of intermediality is not the technologically generated illusion, but the participant's perception of the gaps among the media that generate the illusion (Cegys 2020: 84; and see Boenisch 2006). These gaps require VR participants to engage actively in meaning-making in a way that is cognate, perhaps, with the witnessing that Freddie Rokem says constitutes an active self-reflection on one's 'role and experience as a spectator' (2010), or the active 'inhabiting' of representational worlds that Robin Ridington describes as the role of the listener in Indigenous storytelling (1998). When it uses impressionism to generate intermediality, VR may be less a mechanical or even an embodied concern, and more a perceptual concern, which invites us to understand participant agency as a form of self-reflection arising out of the 'affective dissonance' that Roger Simon argues is 'significant for either confirming or altering one's framework for acting in the world' (2011). An increasing body of theoretical work on virtuality is acknowledging the participant's perception as the medium in

---

[6] See *ImagineNative 2167 VR tour* (2018–19).

[7] See *ImagineNative 2167 VR tour* (2018–19).

which the virtual manifests (e.g. Grimshaw 2014). If we were to conceive of Shakespeare in VR as 'immersive experiences delivered through the human imagination' (Damer and Hinrichs 2013), beholden to the standards established in a millennia-long history of 'virtual art' in a range of earlier media (Grau 2003), we might expect and enable it to demand the same critical and ethical engagements that we expect of everything else we call 'art', including 'Shakespeare'.

Proposition 3: Like Shakespeare, VR engages spectators in communal acts of meaning-making. Rather than generating individualised experiences, it generates opportunities for the communal consideration of shared experiences.

The community-building, meaning-making power of watching others watch the stage was an integral aspect of early modern theatrical experience (Dawson and Yachnin 2005). On my first visit to a VR arcade, what struck me most vividly was the way in which each VR participant was similarly a spectacle for others watching. Some commercial VR experiences have capitalised on the potential of VR as a spectator sport so successfully that it is arguably more fun to watch other people play than to play yourself (see *Richie's Plank Experience* for a vivid example). But the principle extends to the full range of extant applications of VR: ultimately, if it is the experience of the VR participant that is of interest, it is of interest not only to each participant individually, but also to the community (or communities) to which the participant belongs.

In the same way that no individual game can constrain the gameplay of its players (Boluk and LeMieux 2017), no individual VR build can constrain the experience of its participants. As in the theatre, the meaning of a VR experience is located outside, not inside, the 'magic circle' that has come to be understood as the hermetic space of a virtual world (e.g. Salen and Zimmerman 2003). It lives more substantively in the discourses that arise from it than in the experience itself, and it will continue to be co-constituted by discursive communities long after the technologies that originally generated it have become obsolete. For us as teachers of 'Shakespeare', this matters because it confirms that the discourses we generate through the use of VR in our classrooms will shape the social spheres in which students engage long after our classes have ended. This final proposition about what

Shakespeare has to offer VR, then, makes explicit the question that under-
lies the preceding two – namely, to what end are we teaching 'Shakespeare'
at all? It engages us in precisely the kinds of critical and ethical questions
that technological monomania, utopianism, and determinism dodge, by
asking us not what we can do, but why, and how we will hold ourselves
accountable.

Shakespearean VR

My proposal, in summary, is that Shakespeare might do quite a lot for VR.
In particular, I propose that we Shakespeare educators need not think of
ourselves as beneficiaries of the affordances of a revolutionary new technology. Instead, we might think of ourselves as contributors to the development of the discursive spaces occupied by the audiences for this new
medium. As Harry Robert Wilson has recently observed, other aesthetic
applications of virtual reality do just that; virtual reality performance, for
example, 'challenges the promise of VR . . . to provide unmediated presence
and immersion by drawing attention to attention, defamiliarizing our everyday perceptions, foregrounding media of representation, their aesthetics
and techniques – drawing us in and pushing us away' (2020: 130).

In its emphasis on the self-reflexivity that is enabled when media of
representation are acknowledged and interrogated, Wilson's observation
invokes the metatheatricality so frequently associated with the Shakespearean
theatre. When we acknowledge that our understanding is perceptual and
contingent upon representation, we can begin to understand ourselves as
members of discursive communities engaged in shared meaning-making.
What if, as educators and producers, we imagined the virtuality of VR not
in terms of the affordances of a closed technological system that generates
hermetic illusions, but as an encounter with alternate, perhaps not actual, but
certainly possible, versions of the real? What if we asked of it what we ask of
aesthetic works in other media – what we ask of 'Shakespeare' in fact – which is
to help us to reflect not just on what our experiences mean, but also on how we
have come to ascribe those meanings, and what their consequences might be?

If 'Shakespeare in VR' has been, to date, a stable rendering of something
easily recognisable as a work of Shakespeare within the affordances of
emerging VR technologies, 'Shakespearean VR' is the potential generation

of everything we haven't yet thought of as Shakespeare in the minds of unique participants, prompted by an unpredictable range of established and emerging media. Three new design precepts for developing Shakespearean VR may help us to achieve that potential.

1. Because VR experiences are located in the perceptions of participants, they can be open systems.
2. Virtual reality experiences offer the greatest potential to enable participants' interpretive agency when they open up intermedial spaces for engagement.
3. Virtual reality experiences have the greatest potential to effect positive social change when they embrace and encourage communal experience and reflection.

Understood as a 'Shakespearean' medium, VR has the potential to enable open aesthetic systems of interaction among media and discursive communities, systems that can be leveraged to help us to engage our students in the values that underlie our pedagogy. So long as VR reaches for openness in the aesthetic experiences it generates, it will be Shakespearean; the greater its openness, the more Shakespearean it will be – and as it becomes more Shakespearean, it will become increasingly able to hold us accountable for actualising the better realities it helps us to imagine.

2 'As We Are [Hacked] with Art':
The Shakespearean Imagination in the Virtual Age
Scott Hollifield

In the reflection of Jennifer Roberts-Smith's essential query lurks a doppelgänger: *What has Shakespeare done for virtual reality (VR)?* The immediate response is perhaps not as enigmatic as it seems. Alongside such nascent cinematic technologies as the zoetrope and kinetoscope, we can credit Shakespeare as arch-collaborator in the ways Western audiences hear and process dialogue, connect sound and image, navigate between images, and construct expectations of dramatic scale. With keen awareness of the auditor's imaginative faculties, Shakespeare fostered the illusion that two senses (those easiest to take for granted and most subject to degradation) could at their nexus stand for all five. The interconnectedness of Shakespeare with modern visual narrative transcends direct adaptations of canonical works and the most literary-minded appropriations of Shakespearean tropes. Where R. S. White has shown that the formation and codification of romantic genres in early Hollywood owed a debt to Shakespeare, I suggest that Shakespeare may also have influenced how twentieth-century cinema – and twenty-first-century virtual reality – would be consumed by viewers.

Users of the coin-operated kinetoscope paid a nickel each to become the camera eye itself, agents of perception in technological circumstances more or less under their control. As the makers of perceived motion, spectators became authors of the moving images on view despite not having created them, like a playwright adapting an extant source or a film editor assembling a coherent sequence from irreconcilable footage. Like those early perceivers of the moving image, our experience of the visual world is as informed by mechanical technologies and content delivery systems as by the stuff of visual storytelling; like auditors of early modern performance, our Shakespearean imaginations rely upon a contractual compromise of agency and self, facilitating potential enhancements to both.

These negotiations of sound and vision appear to prefigure the conceptual ideals of VR: user-attuned, fully immersive, endlessly adaptable. And yet even the most thoughtful and immersive VR must hijack the senses and imaginations of its participants. The delivery system itself undermines the sensory and intellectual exchanges its content demands, creating experience-less experience, not unlike a sinister dream that prefers a passive receptor to an active subconscious. Posing a quandary both frightening and intriguing, however, research suggests that VR experiences can produce actual, enduring memories of lived experience. Researchers, attempting to distinguish 'episodic' from 'autobiographical' memories, found these terms insufficient to describe data collected and patterns observed.[8] The field now deploys the longer-to-retrieve 'participation-based memory' (PBM) and the less detail-oriented 'observation-based memory' (OBM) as its operative terms (Rubin 2018: 141).

Shakespearean drama, through specific characters or 'agents', makes strategic appeals to both types of memory, offering imaginative prescriptions for engaging them. While resonating with mechanisms of cinema, these elements also productively mirror the internalising/externalising mechanics of emerging VR technologies. Following White's suggestion that 'Shakespearean' conceptions of genre informed the development of narrative cinema, I contend that the basic cinematic apparatus embraces a distinctly Shakespearean point of view. With VR, the more overtly cinematic aspects can be seen to invert that point of view: the unflinching gaze, rather than reflecting the user's actual self, converts their consciousness into a self-generating simulation. To illuminate these notions, let's consider an intriguing pair of Shakespearean agents, each a harbinger of the virtual world and its intersections with the real.

The Shakespearean Hacking Consciousness: Mercutio

Envisioning immersive virtual reality in *Neuromancer*, William Gibson coined the concept of 'consensual hallucination' as an ideal VR state. As Jeremy Bailenson notes in his summary of Gibson's view, 'It will be the

---

[8] Episodic memories entail an awareness of the continuity of the self over time. Autobiographical memories are similar because they also centre on personal information, but they do not entail the same subjective awareness (Rubin 2018: 141).

community of people interacting within [the Matrix]' rather than 'graphics or photorealistic avatars' that will '[bring] the world alive through the mutual acknowledgement of its reality' (Bailenson 2018: 174). Mercutio's Queen Mab speech is a corrective, participation-based simulation intended (until it backfires on its conjuror) to drive a wedge of distinction between Romeo's illusions of Love – themselves simulations created during Romeo's acts of reading, self-reinforced in his moments of oral composition – and the sexual desire he prefers to weigh down with lead. Romeo cultivates isolation and invites darkness, gestures of the Petrarchan lover's self-imposed asceticism. Further, the 'misshapen chaos of well-seeming forms' that Benvolio interprets as 'oppression' suggests to Mercutio a profound need for immersive simulation (1.1.177, 182).[9]

Mercutio stands among Shakespeare's earliest attempts to draw an audience from fixed positions of bench seat and standing room into an intimate, tactile world as it comes to life. A Shakespearean agent who projects his consciousness into another character, Mercutio delivers a fantastical message beyond the play's dramatic needs. Like a prologue to the as-yet unheard and unseen, Mercutio seems as keen on educating ears and expanding minds as he is on engaging in sophisticated, highly sexualised banter. He requires only arcane knowledge, above-par verbal dexterity, and Romeo's receptive imagination to plant this dream and see it thrive. Yet Mercutio builds this ethereal realm of so many concrete details – 'an empty hazelnut', worms 'pricked' from lazy maid-fingers, 'a tithe-pig's tail'– that he finds himself as circumscribed by the physical world as he expects Romeo to be among the twists of his fantasia (1.4.59, 68–9, 79).

Accepting the audiovisual components of VR experience as descendants of narrative cinema, let's consider the Queen Mab speech in cinematic terms. Mercutio narrows depth of field and restricts the frame, not unlike a rudimentary VR headset or the viewfinder of a kinetoscope. Developed for Thomas Edison circa 1889 by William Kennedy Dickson, the kinetoscope was a peephole viewer that allowed a spectator to view sequential images on revolving celluloid sheets. The fixed yet immersive point of view

---

[9] For further analysis of the immersive and simulative qualities of the Queen Mab speech, see Spellberg 2013.

originally afforded by the Dickson kinetoscope is the opposite of the head-on-a-swivel, 'open-world' subjectivities invited by early modern public theatregoing. Through such a viewfinder, a participant may explore the edges and contents of the frame but – like Romeo in Mercutio's imaginative thrall – he cannot enter or navigate the spaces he observes. While typically top-mounted and down-facing, the kinetoscope peephole approximated forward-facing, proscenium-rooted sightlines. By banishing the peripheral, however, this promising device (not unlike early VR headsets) revealed the limits of its vision in short order. Conjuring a virtual headset for Romeo, Mercutio stages another kind of play within a play – nearly a frame within a frame – for the attuned auditor. His faerie vision steepens the imagination's learning curve, offering glimpses into other worlds, other logics beyond the play's stage-bound conceits, such as:

> Her traces of the smallest spider web,
> Her collars of the moonshine's watery beams,
> Her whip of cricket's bone, the lash of film
> [. . .]
> And in this state she gallops night by night
> Through lovers' brains (1.4.64–71)

Within this elaborate tableau, Mercutio directs eyes and ears to its uncanniest details, somehow appealing to the senses all at once. Like a peephole viewer, he delimits the frame of this dream vision before projecting Romeo into it, allowing limited freedom to pan, tilt, and scan within these mediated close-ups. Only from this formally fixed position, like the VR observer oppressed by goodly gear and participation anxiety, can Mercutio step-zoom Romeo line by line into Mab's microcosmos.

Ensuring a pliant receiver, Mercutio immobilises Romeo before hijacking his higher faculties, sharing his perceptions via live feed. This approach, not necessarily intended by its developers, is embodied in Dickson's evolving design for the kinetoscope. Among the earliest means of programmatic escapism, this technology offered a semi-private screening experience with the illusion of cinematographic control. This arrangement also appears to predict the viewer's proximity to illusion in a VR headset: to experience technological wonder, insert head here. Modern VR lifts these inherent limitations through 360-degree modelling, increased pixel density, and high frame and refresh rates; some systems, however, threaten the threshold of what our optic nerves and visual imaginations can actually process. As Jaron Lanier puts it, 'When we think technology can surpass our bodies in a comprehensive way, we are forgetting what we know about our bodies and physical reality' (2017: 49). Beyond this, even the most seamless simulacrum cannot provide the freedom of moving one's head to better orient one's ears and eyes. In such a consensual hallucination, agency and reality are only ever illusions. Presenting a 'team of little atomi' drawn 'over men's noses as they lie asleep', Mercutio negates the focal distance between invited observer and evoked object (1.4.57–8). Microscopic entities held up to the eye need not be magnified in the imagination, thus skipping the very moment of perception.

If sight and sound are essential to effective simulation (and, in reverse order, to early modern drama in performance), then touch (by way of haptic devices and unforced interactivity) represents a potentially productive third sense in VR. Mercutio dwells on points of contact between Mab's miniscule entourage and the knees, lips, and necks that careful auditors might imagine her hazelnut chariot to transit. Yet he emphasises fingers foremost among sense organs, eyes being closed and ears largely dormant whilst the dreamer dreams. Like the brain matter she gallops through, or an effective VR simulation's programmed audiovisual stimuli, the senses remain in thrall: the noses Mab tickles don't smell, lips erupt in sores but don't taste or kiss, fingers feel but don't actively touch. When she does engage eardrums, synchronising dream with waking world, Mab disrupts and reconfigures both.

The effect of Mercutio's speech is consistent with the visual provenance Shakespeare so often assigns the aural faculties. His words' specific impacts on ears suggest the equilibrium, spatial awareness, time-sense, and visual content of dreams as determined or supplemented by sound, especially waking world noises appropriated and repurposed by the dreaming subconscious. Neither suggesting possibility nor presenting for interpretation, he imposes his mind's contents upon Romeo's senses. In a sequence relatively ungoverned by early modern theatrical practice, Mercutio seems content to disrupt Romeo's spiritual equilibrium, lightening his 'soul of lead' (1.4.15) with an ethereal world's microcosmic details. Rather than slowing his body or fixing it in space, Romeo's soul must learn to transcend such earthly anchors as Love. Rather than locking his mind into a rigid Petrarchan box step, that soul must rediscover its origins as an animating, engendering force, elevated to an objective, observational state on Mercutian gusts of imagery.

Mercutio opens a gateway between the polarities of Shakespearean performance received and VR experience imposed. Putting his best fever dream forward to reprogramme Romeo's Petrarchan imagination, Mercutio redirects Love's laser focus from its own constructs to the bio- and neurological essences of tactile sensuality. In this moment, the play's reality becomes organic, messy, and subject to corruption. Through his visceral account of lovers' subconscious fantasies, Mercutio elevates Romeo's spirit from gravity-challenged 'feather of lead' to an expansive, celestial observer (1.1.178). Mercutio's simulation thus divests Romeo of his preoccupation with outward shows and instils an abiding awareness of a lover's cosmic insignificance, further readying him to encounter the earthy, Ovidian Juliet.

Yet Mercutio is an agent of anti-romance, whose protective cynicism briefly diverts Romeo's Petrarchan inclinations from their tragic trajectory, abetting this play's rare ability to induce audiences to forget its predetermined outcomes. This level of synergy, ultimately traceable to an Aristotelian sense of awe, synchronises with narcotic effects of early modern performance illuminated by Tanya Pollard and contagious transmissions of emotion elucidated by Mary Floyd-Wilson (Pollard 2005; Floyd-Wilson 2013: 47–72). In the space between foreknowledge and hope, Mercutio encourages us to imagine less devastating alternatives.

When Mercutio projects his consciousness into Romeo's leaden soul, his reach extends beyond the playhouse stage and into auditing imaginations. Collaborating with attuned playgoers, Shakespeare renders the intangible almost tactile, in this way rivalling the immersive visual effects upon which commercial cinema and games have come to rely. As the film industry has invented imagery to approximate a Shakespearean hold on the active, spectatorial imagination, future VR should strive not to impose virtual imagination but to imagine wholesale: transcend headset and interface, conjure content with Mercutio's maddening intricacy, and emerge from the moment when inquisitive user harmonises with evolving technology. What I suggest is not exactly free-range, open-world VR (which might be impossible given the need to manoeuvre participants towards waypoints), but an elastic horizon of possibility stretched by a level of emotional engagement that at least matches VR's high potential for complete-seeming audiovisual illusions and extensions of the real.

Heralding Hamlet's manifestation as directorial consciousness during 'The Murder of Gonzago', this 'consciousness hack' suggests an emerging Shakespearean paradigm – in which an agent hijacks a character's prevailing mindset – and establishes Mercutio as an embodiment of early modern imagination. Mercutio dabbles; however, Paulina masters this 'hacking' effect: projecting the play's moment of wonder through Leontes, she ultimately accesses any attuned auditing consciousness in range (onstage or off), hacking *The Winter's Tale* itself. Where Mercutio's Mab speech is a simulation act, Paulina becomes a conduit of Shakespearean simulation, directing Leontes' senses and perception, resetting and reframing audience reception on the fly, and broadcasting a blushing-painted, living-dead Hermione in real time.

Shakespeare's Virtual Priestess: Paulina

Paulina is *The Winter's Tale*'s primary source of wonder. She does not simply survive a Jacobean play in which a paranoid tyrant repeatedly calls for punishment by fire and brands her 'a mankind witch', 'hag', and 'crone' in a single scene (2.3.67, 2.3.107, 2.3.76). Paulina elicits trust (even devotion) from that tyrant, whose curses rested primarily upon her ability to mediate her passions with reason. Mentoring Leontes into repentance, she becomes the custodian of that which will ultimately save him: Hermione's memory. Paulina plants these experimental memories ahead of their time, in the back of the king's mind, tends them in the cool, dark space between Acts Three and Four, and grooms her penitent to absorb their full, epiphanic impact. Sicilia's former rejections of obvious truths – a wife's fidelity, a bosom friend's responsibilities, his own paternity – and the suffering they engender overcome his monolithic will. Once incapable of giving credence to true things, Leontes now sees only opposites of false: the same observational imagination that contrived Hermione's infidelity ultimately insists on the authenticity of her stone likeness.

Shakespeare empowered Paulina to nurture the king's blessed-cursed imagination, but also trusted his evolving playhouse audience to engage the performance at an advanced level. Mirroring the many divided consciousnesses of *The Winter's Tale* (Leontes is both king and pilgrim, Paulina avenger and re-educator, Perdita shepherdess and princess), the audience maintains an observational remove as the play translates individual auditors into subjective participants. If the scene is to transcend expectation and inspire awe, each auditor must adopt the king's point of view even as they objectively witness his rapture. Awareness dawns, adjunct to these imaginative interactions, that a character has unburdened the playwright of the play's reins. Paulina cultivates her auditors' double employment as accessories and witnesses to Leontes' rehabilitation, readying them to encounter a miracle through his eyes.

A character in an early modern romance, not a genre revered for narrative plausibility or emotional realism, teaches the play's central character and audience how to see (and believe) beyond the visual. Though Paulina arises as the primary voice of reason in *The Winter's Tale*, no precise semblance of Paulina appears in Shakespeare's likely narrative sources.[10] The philosophy she imparts to Leontes, however, advocates an existential truth arrived at by emotional, rather than rational, interpretation. Since her earlier scenes amount to impassioned but logical defences of Hermione and robust but carefully considered appeals to kingly wisdom, it may help to consider Paulina's offstage action while Time 'slide[s] / O'er sixteen years, and leave[s] the growth untried / Of that wide gap' (4.1.5–7).

Turning her persistent critique of courtly advice towards the practical, she keeps Leontes in widowers' weeds for the duration. While

---

[10] Robert Greene's *Pandosto*, Euripides' *Alcestis*, and the Pygmalion myth are traditionally identified as Shakespeare's narrative touchstones for *The Winter's Tale*. See John Pitcher's introduction ('Tragedy into Romance,' 10–24), the note for 'Paulina' in the list of roles (141, n. 9), and 'Sources' (405–52) in the Arden 3.

Cleomenes and Dion suggested that Hermione's replacement would heal Leontes and Sicily, Paulina contends that the only way to make the kingdom whole is to resolve the troubling consequences of the king's actions. These include not only his treatment of Hermione, the alienation of Polixenes, and the deaths of Antigonus and Mamillius, but the damage Leontes has wrought upon himself. Rather than ensure he suffers as he deserves, Paulina represses a justifiable urge for vengeance, averting the implicit tragedy of *Pandosto* and *Alcestis*. Instead, in the tradition of medieval romance, she brings an errant man under benevolent control, channelling their mutual griefs into his rapturous conversion. Under Paulina's tutelage, Leontes reacquires his ability to listen and develops the elusive sixth sense called insight. In addition to her primary mission, which included keeping Hermione secreted away for sixteen years, Paulina remains the sole custodian of the Apollonian prophecy. Leontes suffers for having contravened the oracle, but his personal undoing of those wrongs is not demanded.

Through Paulina, Shakespeare generates a stunning, unparalleled instance of audience empathy. Though his romances each seem to strive towards resolutions both devastating and sublime, we cannot call the effect catharsis. Its interests are liminal, neither local nor global but situated at junctions of stage and audience, preoccupied with moments that arise between two sides of an argument. With nothing less wondrous than the realignment of Sicilia's stars in her charge, even Paulina must call up reinforcements. As the Chorus of *Henry V* relies upon the 'imaginary forces' of his theatrical audience, Paulina produces further seeds of wonder at 5.1.102 (calling the Gentleman out for the 'shrewdly ebbed' quality of his verse). The Gentleman, in turn, sows those seeds in the following scene, reporting to Autolycus the fragmentary amazements he has witnessed. Recalling the revelation of Perdita's identity and its aftermath, he muses of Leontes and the exiled lord Camillo:

> They seemed almost, with staring on one another, to tear
> the cases of their eyes. There was speech in their dumbness,
> language in their very gesture. They looked as they had heard
> of a world ransomed, or one destroyed. A notable passion of wonder

appeared in them, but the wisest beholder, that knew no more
but seeing, could not say if th'importance were joy or sorrow.
(5.2.11–18)

These seeds of wonder germinate in Rogero's and the Steward's
reports of Paulina's 'poor' secluded house; protracted by the tension
of joy and sorrow, they unfold their tendrils away from the palace and
into the gallery housing 'the queen's picture' (5.2.171). While Paulina
has sixteen years of preparation invested in this moment, the playhouse
audience requires a concise bringing-up-to-speed. The collective
retelling and assessment of Leontes and Perdita's reunion can be
read as a blueprint for audience response to the following scene.
Though descended from the mystery play tradition, this third-person
displacement of Leontes' reunions with Perdita and Polixenes ultimately makes dramatic sense. Any staging of the scene would force
players to describe in dialogue emotions typically earmarked for
soliloquy, supplanting contemplation with commentary on what their
characters do not yet understand. Placing the audience in a position to
doubt what they have seen, played before an assembly of onstage
avatars, no less, would undermine Paulina's objective – to hit
Leontes with overwhelming, instantaneous, and very public revelation. Averting such an anticlimax, Shakespeare repolarises the theatrical senses with a shift to oral narrative mode, encouraging ears to
overtake eyes at the threshold of meaning. When Paulina draws
a curtain to reveal her Romano-sculpted likeness of Hermione, she
restores visual balance to the play. Leontes, however, finds himself
entirely spellbound by the visual. As the previously still figure steps
down from the plinth, onstage and playhouse worlds harmonise; still
comprehending Hermione as simulacrum, each spectator gropes for
reason through heightened senses and finds only the surge of emotion
(5.3.109–14).

In this Shakespearean prediction of the virtual epiphany, in the blink
before she rejoins the 'real', the apotheosis of everything 'Hermione'
materialises in the fleeting hive-mind that links Leontes with his auditors.
More than four centuries after the fact, Paulina's resurrection of Hermione

remains exceptional among illusory moments: the audience knows that what it sees, though they experience it, is not happening now in their specific space and time. And yet somehow, they might be content to suffer eternity in such a moment. This revelation hoists the bar of theatrical wonder so high that only technological magic (or virtual replacements of the senses) might produce the illusion of topping it. The downside is that many worthy entertainments, falling short of this mark, strike the once-blessed spectator as underwhelming. If a theatrical moment can underwhelm, then it cannot resonate with an audience's sense of the real. As the simulation forsakes the individual observer when it must emphasise an objective, or packs the frame with more than eye can see or cerebral cortex can process, the possibility of such moments as these, let alone the subjective perceptions, sensations, and emotions they might produce, decreases exponentially.

At the peak of its collective powers, early modern drama (abetted by a willing, engaged audience) bent well-worn hyperreal tropes into imaginative hyper-realities, the facets on the fringe of Hamlet's 'mirror up to nature' or the glass in *Macbeth*'s show of kings. Among his most profound contributions to Western culture, Shakespeare's verbal-to-visual effects create meaningful polarities of emotion and imagination. In performance, plays as disparate as *Romeo and Juliet* and *The Winter's Tale* expand stage-bound illusion into the theatrical space while inviting their audiences of attuned collaborators to determine the limits of those proto-virtual realities.

Despite the activity implicit in 'screening', 'watching', or even 'binge-ing', spectatorship remains a passive – but potentially experiential – activity. While our experience of and engagement with visual forms of storytelling have shaped our sensory expectations of virtual worlds, the spontaneous physical interactions that make them feel real are likely to interrupt a carefully crafted simulation. Beyond the aural faculties, effective virtual realities must, like the most fully realised cinematic experiences, engage not only the sense of sight, but aural-visual memory and imagination. It should also be noted that cinematic interactions with the senses of smell and touch, virtually impossible through the ears no matter how evocative the poetry, are most likely to begin with the eyes.

Rather than sow mere seeds of ideas, Mercutio and Paulina transplant fully formed images into the attuned auditing imagination. Like an ideal visual object, from sculpture to fresco to cinematic frame, such a Shakespearean image thrives on interpretive flexibility. The cinematic image, however, can achieve a realism that sidelines the interpretive imagination, a mode cultivated in recent popular film-making. Therapeutic applications aside, this seems destined to become the default mode of commercially minded VR. Physical passivity may be a desirable – even ideal – state for a mass audience, but deliberate engenderings of intellectual, emotional, or imaginative passivity seem to loudly herald human devolution.

II Education

3 *Virtual Reality in the Classroom*
David McInnis

English mountaineer George Mallory famously responded to the question of why he wanted to climb Mount Everest with the glib reply, 'Because it's there.' We live in a period when access to multimedia technologies has never been cheaper or more readily available, but *should* we be using virtual reality, 360-degree filming, and other modes of filming in the Shakespearean classroom simply *because they're there*? How might these modes of engagement with Shakespeare enhance our pedagogical practices? In this section I reflect on the challenges and limitations of two recent projects in which I used 360 filming to produce multimedia assets for teaching Shakespeare at the University of Melbourne. The first, a 360 video of the final scene of *The Taming of the Shrew*, was produced as part of a suite of resources for a blended-learning approach to teaching and sits alongside a number of other scenes from Shakespeare filmed by more conventional means. The second is the assassination scene from *Julius Caesar*, produced as part of the transmedia production *#ItWasGreekToMe*, associated with 'Major Hack', a humanities hackathon run by the university in July 2019.

360° Shrew

'ENGL20033: Shakespeare in Performance' is currently the only unit entirely dedicated to Shakespeare in the undergraduate curriculum at the University of Melbourne. Consequently, a great deal is at stake. Enrolments consist primarily of students who have not necessarily studied Shakespeare before, or have only done so from a literary studies perspective. As such, a vital aspect of the pedagogy is attention to both blended and active learning. Accordingly, in class, students are encouraged to get up on their feet and undertake a variety of performance exercises that improve their understanding of how staging choices create critical interpretations. They work through key scenes of the plays and critique archival footage (often rare or unique) of those same scenes, to better develop an understanding of the difference performance makes. Two weeks are spent on each play, and one to two small groups of students will perform a scene in the second week of the fortnight, demonstrating their understanding of how to create meaning through embodied experience.

The Taming of the Shrew is a fabulous play to start a course with because it is so fraught and highly charged; ostensibly a 'comedy' (students need to understand that term historically), it's actually very disturbing for modern audiences. As even people who have never seen the play know, the final scene of *The Taming of the Shrew* is notoriously problematic. Does Katharina willingly submit to Petruchio? Does she submit at all? I ask students to consider three possibilities: that the play is a farce, and therefore ends as a farce (and Kate's speech is ironic); that the Christopher Sly Induction is irrelevant, so the ending is literal (because Kate has been tamed, broken down, recognises an equal match in Petruchio, etc.); or that the play is open-ended. Perhaps more so than any other scene in the play, these final moments contain the greatest potential to be affected by production decisions. In 2015, the Melbourne University Shakespeare Company (a student group that produces up to two plays per year with different student directors and actors) produced *Shrew*, directed by Fiona Spitzkowsky. With funding I received in the form of a Teaching and Learning Initiatives grant from the Faculty of Arts, I was able to pay the student actors and director and to enlist the professional assistance of the Faculty's eTeaching team's camera crew and post-production suite. We filmed the final scene three times, in three different ways, to showcase significantly different production decisions. The first, 'sitcom' version (www.vimeo.com/170713376), was described as follows by the director:

> The scene is presented in the same hand-held, rough cut style similar to talking head sitcoms like *The Office* and *Parks and Recreation* to support a light-hearted interpretation of an otherwise harshly phrased monologue, with the quick cuts and reaction shots allowing the actors to reveal that the characters, particularly the male characters, do not always believe what they're saying. (Spitzkowsky, director's notes)

In the second, 'tableau' version (www.vimeo.com/170711675), the scene 'is filmed in a very stylized manner, informed and inspired by *The Stepford Wives*, *Desperate Housewives* and soap operas. It is melodramatic in its framing, colour scheme and performances to evoke a sense of a controlled and cloying culture of attrition and submission' (Spitzkowsky). The students watch both of these versions of the final scene before coming to class; in class, I distribute a class set of Google Cardboard VR viewers (affordable, foldable headsets made from cardboard, designed to enable VR experiences with smartphones) so they can watch the third, 360° version. Although I am fortunate to have access to a full class set of these viewers – in 2016, as part of our Shakespeare400 programme of events, we invested in hundreds of University-branded viewers and distributed them to all secondary schools in the state of Victoria – there are still students who are unable to watch the 360 footage because they do not own a compatible smartphone. Extra time must therefore be allocated to the exercise so students can swap with their neighbours or use a viewer that contains my own phone.

In the 360 version directed by Spitzkowsky and Declan Mulcahy, and produced by Jason O'Leary (www.youtube.com/watch?v=1UcDK2pQIY8; best watched with a VR headset, using the YouTube app and the split-screen mode), the audience is not so much a fly on the wall (an outsider, uninvolved) as they are right in the thick of the action: the multiple GoPro cameras we used to record the scene were positioned on a tripod in the middle of the set. The scene was filmed in a kitchen (reinforcing the director's vision for the play as a dark commentary on domestic abuse), with characters circulating around the stationary audience member. In the live stage version, the audience sat on all four sides of a kitchen set, with windows behind them, so that they felt they were 'in the room' if not in the very centre; a knife block was positioned suggestively in the centre of the kitchen (recalling Chekhov's gun principle; it was not, however, finally used in the denouement of the play, which remained technically a 'comedy' in not ending in bloodshed). Beyond the novelty value of the 360 viewing, the technological approach is meant to complement the artistic interpretation: as the audience is immersed and immobile, they recognise their complicity in the domestic abuse unfolding before them. Unable to intervene but also unable to move, students are confronted with a difficult decision about their attention: some focus on Katharina as she delivers her final speech, some prefer to focus on the reactions of other characters, others tend to avoid eye contact altogether and focus on inanimate objects or look at their own 'feet' (amusingly, if one does look directly down whilst wearing the headsets, one sees a barstool rather than feet. We had next to no budget!). In all three versions of the final scene, the camera work and acting styles change without otherwise altering the dialogue, setting, or actors, in order to prompt discussion of performance choices and their power to affect interpretation. This alignment of directorial vision and technological possibility invariably proves strongly affective and helps students to appreciate how the many variables of a live performance can shape their experience of a play.

It is not, however, an experiment that I have contemplated reprising in subsequent weeks of the semester. For one thing, although recreating a bloody battlefield in *Macbeth* might be moderately thrilling and entertaining, I cannot justify it pedagogically; the novelty of the medium would detract from the purpose of teaching. Also, and importantly, there are physical and perhaps ableist concerns to consider: a number of students report that the experience prompts motion sickness, is disorienting, or simply doesn't work if they have vision-related challenges. For another, there are pragmatic reasons not to repeat the experiment: I typically have to devote a full thirty minutes to the viewing of a ten-minute VR clip because students (despite the myth of digital nativity) require assistance using the Vimeo or YouTube apps, finding the video, setting up the Google Cardboard headsets, and adjusting to the experience of watching the clip. Even if students opt not to watch the entire ten minutes of the clip – I do emphasise that it's not strictly necessary to watch the entirety; the point is more to consider how a purportedly passive observer can nonetheless be rendered complicit and play an active role in the spectacle they witness – it is still a time-consuming exercise.

#ItWasGreekToMe

The second experience I had with VR/360 filming of Shakespeare for classroom purposes had a different target demographic and purpose. As part of the 2019 external marketing and recruitment activity for our

Bachelor of Arts degree, my colleague Jason O'Leary (with a background in theatre and the creative arts) orchestrated a humanities hackathon ('Major Hack'; www.ba.unimelb.edu.au/majorhack) revolving around the death of Julius Caesar. Hackathons are typically associated with coding or the sciences; they present students with a challenge to solve in groups, culminating in their presentation of solutions. This hackathon was for prospective Arts students. It took place over two days on campus and involved between fifty and one hundred sixteen-year-olds. On the first day, the students were given multiple perspectives on Caesar: I spoke about the purpose and politics of Shakespeare's play for an Elizabethan audience; colleagues spoke about the historical Caesar (Classics), about political coups (Politics), about the transmission of news through ballads (History), and about fake news (Media and Communications). Students were then given their prompt: in the wake of Caesar's assassination, they had to decide whose side they were on (Caesar's followers or the conspirators) and develop a marketing campaign for their chosen cause. But in the lead-up to the on-campus experience, students engaged in a transmedia production of Shakespeare's *Julius Caesar* (called *#ItWasGreekToMe*), developed and directed by O'Leary with acting students from the Victorian College of the Arts (the Creative Arts Faculty of the University of Melbourne). Users signed up to receive notifications from a Facebook Messenger bot (www.m.me/ItWasGreekToMe) and were subsequently drip-fed videos, intercepted chats and Skype calls, redacted scripts, surveillance footage and a VR experience of the assassination scene (www.vimeo.com/345610516/476d0df048).

Although there was arguably some intrinsic value in filming the assassination scene (specifically) in an immersive manner (this time only 180° was used, not 360°), it had less to do with creating a virtual presence that would implicate the audience. The violence was necessarily stylised and toned down for the adolescent audience and educational context, leaving only residual shock at being virtually present to witness multiple conspirators stab Caesar in the back (whilst other characters, soaking up the scandal, pulled out their mobile phones to broadcast news of the assassination to the outside world). Perhaps a larger cast or more physical obstacles to obtaining a clear view of the violence would have enhanced the sense of chaos for the virtual audience and generated stronger affect (or at least confusion). As things stood, I wasn't entirely convinced that the immersive filming felt all that immersive – more widescreen (but still flat / fourth wall).

What the immersive filming *did* do, however, was to punctuate the stream of multimedia assets with something unique and arresting, appropriately drawing attention to this as the pivotal scene in the production and the hackathon. A series of 'intercepted' chats and 'leaked' audio recordings (etc.) served their purpose, but this scene alone was filmed in this manner. As such, its use of technology seems defensible to me, but the greater value of the transmedia production (to which this scene contributes without stealing the show) is the creation of a sense of an unfolding, imminent conspiracy. Unlike a traditional stage production of *Caesar*, this production played out over a period of days and positioned the audience to feel isolated rather than part of a collective viewing experience; audience members received individual scenes as if they were occurring in real time and a political coup was brewing. Antony's eulogy for Caesar – the galvanising speech that set in train the events that follow and thus provided the impetus for the students to develop their marketing/communications strategy – took the form of a 'live' Instagram video and was timed to release whilst the students were physically grouped together for dinner on campus at the end of day one of the hackathon.

Anecdotally, I think the hackathon and associated transmedia production were a success inasmuch as they seemed to genuinely engage the target demographic. Whether we harnessed the distinguishing features of VR and leveraged them for unique advantages or whether the success of the assassination scene may be attributable to reserving one media format for exclusive use in that crucial scene is harder to tell.

Despite my reservations about the limitations of the uses of immersive/ VR filming, both ended up receiving media coverage. The 360 *Shrew* was featured on commercial television in a segment on the evening news, as part of their coverage of the University's Open Day, as an example of something old (Shakespeare) / something new (VR) converging. A short public engagement piece I wrote (www.pursuit.unimelb.edu.au/articles/friends-romans-fake-news) following the hackathon, about how Shakespeare and an Arts education can foster critical thinking skills, led to an interview (on a national radio station) that was more about the transmedia *Caesar* than the value of an Arts education. In other words, there is clearly an appetite for pedagogical uses of VR and similar technologies: the public, at least, thinks this is what we should be doing more of (or, at the very least, the novelty is headline-worthy). Moreover, in the course of working with a national Shakespeare company in Australia – the Bell Shakespeare Company – I've been privy to conversations about the demand for cheap but scholarly uses of VR in regional classrooms. So there are access and equity considerations at play, not just novelty.

Were VR to become more common in the classroom, I suggest it would be on account of the fact that empowering students to explore Shakespeare for themselves is crucial and is something VR is well-equipped to facilitate. Active methods in the classroom help to dispel myths of cultural elitism and encourage students to make Shakespeare their own, resulting in stronger student motivation (Gibson 1998: 11). By repositioning the spectator as agent (immersed, whether active or passive), VR helps consolidate the sense of the open and the generative, choice and variety, rather than foreclosing interpretive possibilities or subordinating the student's response to four centuries of literary criticism (Gibson 1998: 23). Such multimedia helps to move us away from transmission of received wisdom to a more collaborative learning experience in which students play a vital and prominent part (Gibson 1998: 12). Learning is also enhanced simply by providing students with fresh stimuli (in this case, new videos featuring their peers as actors, rather than Hollywood celebrities). Every act of performance is an act of interpretation, and in the case of immersive/interactive videos, each viewing experience will be individual; thus students are already inherently aware that their perceptions of a production are the basis of an interpretation that starts with them. Insomuch as immersive or VR footage encourages users to recognise their role as active participants in the creation of meaning and interpretation, it represents a pedagogically useful advance in technology.

4 Imagination Bodies Forth:
Augmenting Shakespeare with Undergraduates
Emily Bryan

When approaching Shakespeare pedagogy in the college classroom, instructors must choose between two basic approaches: focus on fine-grained interpretation of the text, or focus on interpretation through performance. As a theatre historian and a resident dramaturge at a professional Shakespeare company, I lean into performance-oriented approaches to the plays, getting students up on their feet, staging a scene, showing film and stage productions. I would love nothing more than to pair my 'Introduction to Shakespeare' class with a series of live theatrical productions. However, there are real challenges of time, money, and access to a performance-enhanced curriculum, and for the most part, my students' access to the text is solitary, not in a theatre, but on a phone, and usually without much in the way of critical context or textual glosses. Rather than bemoan the limitations of mobile access to Shakespeare texts, however, I contend that digital distractions can be a productive disruption that helps students to crack open access to Shakespeare and make the text their own. By taking advantage of the opportunities provided by technology, instructors can develop a pedagogy that treats the different ways in which twenty-first-century students 'read' as an asset, rather than a liability.

The Snapchat Generation

Following N. Katherine Hayles' exhortation that we turn from close reading (currently a foundational skill required of undergraduates) to a multiplicity of reading strategies, I have introduced 'augmented annotation' as an assignment in my Shakespeare classes. In *How We Think*, Hayles writes: 'Reading has always been constituted through complex and diverse practices. Now, it is time to rethink what reading is and how it works in the rich mixtures of words and images, sounds and animations, graphics and letters that constitute the environments of twenty-first century literacies' (2012: 80). Hayles advocates for a mixture of close, distant, and machine reading. The crisis in the humanities of students who don't seem to be 'reading', or who are less apt to read long-form or complex texts, is directly addressed by digital humanities scholars like Hayles, Marie-Laure Ryan, Alan Liu, Sharon Marcus, and others, who reimagine reading practices that correspond to the cognitive shift we are experiencing in the age of digital media.

Recognising how deeply embedded our students are in media culture and digital technology, we see what Marshall McLuhan predicted: 'Our human senses, of which all are media extensions, are also fixed charges on our personal energies, and . . . configure the awareness and experience of each one of us' (1994: 21). The notion of media as a cognitive extension seems especially pertinent to the techno-centric culture of the twenty-first century, where the affordances of smartphones and similar devices are intertwined with almost every aspect of peoples' everyday lives. The smartphone is a constant companion – a source of interest, solace, reassurance, anxiety, money, entertainment, and affection. Distributed cognition and extended mind theory provide powerful ways to think about how technology engages with students and vice versa. Evelyn Tribble and John Sutton's work on 'cognitive ecologies' urges critics to consider the ways in which cognitive activities include not only biological, but social, environmental, material, and technological realms (2011). In the classroom, the technologies might include the anthology, the online PDF, SparkNotes, digital images of a manuscript, the laptop, the book, the e-reader, or the cell phone. Collectively, these supplements help to make up a student's extended mind.

Like many teachers, I have accepted the intrusion of the cell phone into my classroom and tried to harness it. The technology of augmented reality (AR) is suited to the concept of distributed cognition because AR mixes and extends reality and imagination. A newer technology than virtual reality, augmented reality overlays a virtual 3D image on an actual space, and students can look through the camera on their phone, see the classroom, and then see 3D objects hovering in space right in front of them. They can choose to curate their 'virtual surroundings'. Unlike virtual reality, augmented reality is not immersive, but applied to an environment. My assignment asked students to overlay images onto text.

Most students have grown up in the age of Snapchat, Instagram, and Pokémon Go with overlaid augmented reality filters integrated into their phones. Yet when I introduced the idea of using an augmented reality app to annotate a piece of text from *A Midsummer Night's Dream*, every student expressed unfamiliarity with augmented reality. Students perceived this as a completely new technology, something 'cool', but 'initially intimidating', even though they all later reported being comfortable using similar technology on Snapchat. Students experienced a dissonance when asked to engage in a literature classroom with technology they associated only with their social lives. Though this kind of visual annotating is not something literary scholars typically engage in, the experience of creating a virtual scene requires students to make interpretive decisions that a literary critic might make in a close reading of a passage. The technology is so imbricated into their lives that they are not aware of it as 'augmented'. Some of this lack of awareness may also be connected to their status as digital natives, a term coined at their birth (nineteen to twenty years ago), as Noam Knoller writes: 'The Post-PC era creates a situation in which we are as much controlled by technology as technology affords us control' (2019: 100). My plan to bring augmented reality to the practice of textual annotation was grounded in 'the physical act of reading in a digital age' (Warwick et al. 2012: 144). With Shakespeare's texts, performance is an integral part of understanding; what if we could use the interactive technology of augmented reality apps to make *reading* Shakespeare more performative? This is not the same as having students 'perform' Shakespeare or even engage with interpreting Shakespeare performances, but rather finding a way to have them perform a kind of 'close reading' by putting Snapchat filters or old-technology 'transparencies' on Shakespeare's texts (Sampaio and Almeida 2016: 898).

My practice was guided by the concept of 'critical making' coined by Matt Ratto and articulated in an article by E. B. Hunter on the video game she created, *Something Wicked* (Hunter 2020; Ratto 2011). As Ratto describes critical making, it 'highlight[s] the reconnection of two modes of engagement with the world that are typically held separate: critical thinking, traditionally understood as conceptually and linguistically based, and physical making, goal-based material work' (www.opendesign now.org/index.html%3Fp=434.html). Though 'critical making' intersects with the maker movement, including 3D printing, engineering, and crafting, Hunter extends Ratto's concept to *digital* critical making. Much like Gina Bloom's game *Play the Knave*, Hunter's *Something Wicked* asks the players to make meaning, creating 'enactive spectatorship' as they play the game (Bloom 2018). 'Enactive' suggests that the spectator is not merely an observer of representational or mimetic play, but feels like they are having an embodied experience, as if they are participating in the process of the game. An important distinction in these gaming and making projects is that the focus is not on the creation of what Ratto calls 'a pedagogical object intended to be experienced by others, but rather the creation of novel understandings of the makers themselves' (2011). The challenge of creating an augmented reality project in the literature classroom is to achieve a kind of 'novel understanding'. In a course *not* designed by a digital humanities scholar with coding experience herself, and *not* designed for computer science majors or people with significant software experience, how can we deploy the technology to 'interface' with Shakespeare's texts and the students in a way that cultivates experiential learning and critical making? Andy Clark optimistically suggests that 'what is special about human brains . . . is precisely their ability to enter into deep and complex relationships with nonbiological constructs, props, and aids' (2003: 5). Is it possible to harness this ability for pedagogical purposes?

Augmenting Shakespeare with Thyng

The goal of this augmented reality assignment was to enhance students' experience of reading complex texts through the use of technology that they might find familiar, but unusual in a classroom setting. I was searching for applications that didn't require extensive knowledge of coding or software engagement beyond what students might do in their own curation of their media lives. Though imperfect as an augmented reality app in ways that I address later, the AR app Thyng (www.thyng.com) provided an easy point of access and enough ease and flexibility of user interface to allow students to work on an 'augmented annotation' and undergo the process-based experience of reading with augmentation, which yielded a digital object they could share with their classmates and me. Students were tasked with taking several lines from *A Midsummer Night's Dream*, creating a text object in AR, and 'annotating' the text with images, video, and animations.

None of the students in the class had experience in graphic design, film editing, or computer science. The range of student projects varied from multimedia organisations of text to simple images, from what Janet H. Murray might call 'narrative microworlds' to clunky artistic renderings (2017: 6). Even in the simplest form, my students experienced what Anne Burdick describes as the 'enhanced means for vivifying and promoting active or experientially augmented modes of engagement' (2012: 48). Students chose any piece of text that they felt was especially rich, dense, or imagistic. They were then required to obtain images of the text, which they could copy from a book or write themselves and upload to the Thyng app.

The library of virtual assets in the Thyng app introduced a number of limitations. Students identified a disconnect between the images provided by Thyng and the text they wanted to bring to life. Images related to Cupid and love seemed trite and inadequate. In Figure 1, the student's discarded effort registers her frustration with the limited images of 'cupidity' in the library of Thyng's assets. The three images hover in space over the student's desk, but the image of cupid as a kind of Betty Boop or kewpie doll really failed to suggest what the student wanted to convey. As this figure suggests, students were inclined to look at Shakespeare's text for the visual images that could be culled, but also texts that lent themselves to overlaying. In placing the antidote to love-in-idleness on Titania's eyes, Oberon speaks this charm:

> Be as thou wast wont to be.
> See as thou wast wont to see.
> Dian's bud o'er Cupid's flower
> Hath such force and blessed power. (4.1.70–3)

In the course of the assignment, many students were drawn to poetic arrangements such as this one, where Shakespeare overlays one image on top of another. Oberon's charm seems to be lifting a veil from Titania's eyes, as if Cupid's flower represents augmented or filtered reality, coaxing Titania to see without the filter as she had seen before. In an anonymous survey after the assignment, students attested to the fact that the difficulties

Figure 1 Annotating *A Midsummer Night's Dream* using the augmented reality application Thyng: limited options for representing 'cupidity'

of working with the app mirrored the frustrations they experienced in close reading. They had to make choices about what to represent visually. Would simply representing Cupid in this passage be sufficient when really the passage references 'Cupid's flower', and how would that be depicted? It led many students to think about how props would be represented on the stage. The transfer to thinking about performance was something that nearly all students mentioned and not something that I had anticipated. I hoped that their reading would be more 'performative', or 'active', but I did not expect it to lead them to think of performance choices. In her essay 'Enactive Spectatorship', Hunter explores the tension in creating the digital 'blood' in her video game adaptation of *Macbeth*, and her experience dealing with the blood as a prop in stage productions of *Macbeth* (2020). Bloom, in her reading of scenes of gaming in early modern plays, recounts a similar phenomenon as the turn to games even in these early plays 'urge[s] a shift to a mode of reading and analysis that we might describe as less semiotic than phenomenological' (2018: 9). The complexity of representing 'Cupid's flower' both as an augmented reality asset and a prop in the theatre coincided in our projects as well. The representation of Cupid's flower in productions of *Dream* are varied and particular: from a potion in a vial, to a giant flower, to beams of light. Without even discussing this significant prop choice as a class, the student engaged in the question herself through her augmented annotation.

My students struggled to find ways to represent words that represented multiple images. In some cases, the augmented annotation sent us back to engage more with the text, not to find a deeper meaning, but to understand the very surface of the text. Hermia's early oath to Lysander, 'I swear to thee by Cupid's strongest bow, / By his best arrow with the golden head' (1.1.169–70) challenged a student who had no experience with the fundamental operation of a bow and arrow. Her augmented annotation focused on a 'golden head' because she found this decadent image of a molten, golden head that completely waylaid her understanding that Hermia meant the head of an arrow. The extravagance of Hermia's love oath was overshadowed by the image the student found, which took the student's understanding of the text in a different direction. Thus an unexpected pedagogical benefit of the exercise was that, although the drive to find suitable images created potential for misunderstanding, it also helped to flag issues with comprehension, allowing for moments of intervention.

Sometimes the proliferation of images and the three-dimensional structure of augmented reality gave the students what they described as a 'visceral' or 'sensory' experience of the passage. For example, one student selected a passage where Titania commands the fairies to attend to Bottom. She says:

> Be kind and courteous to this gentleman.
> Hop in his walks, and gambol in his eyes.
> Feed him with apricots and dewberries,
> With purple grapes, green figs, and mulberries. (*MND*, 3.1.158–61)

The student chose to find images of the fruits mentioned, as seen in Figure 2. In a reflection on the passage and the augmented annotation, the student reported feeling overwhelmed by the presence of 'nature' in the passage and the 'luxuriousness of the fruit, so colorful and varied'.[11] The student wrote: 'Seeing all of the objects mentioned in the text kind of brought it to life, and seeing it was really cool. I felt *like I was in the text* which helped me to understand it better.' Students seemed to experience the text in a different way, not necessarily more deeply thoughtful, but more 'engaged' or energised by what they could figure out about the passage.

This experience also allowed my students to think of themselves differently as readers. They could apply what they understood of themselves as 'visual learners' (a phrase they repeated frequently) and use that as a strength in interpreting literature. Their reflections on the technology and its introduction in class were uniformly positive. One student wrote: 'I think the AR project enhanced my comprehension of the passage I chose. The project encourages you to look at the passage in a different way rather than just reading it. Very cool!' In addition to using a lot of adjectives like 'cool' and 'futuristic', students repeated the idea of augmented annotation as more than 'just reading'. At a moment when English teachers are trying to

---

[11] All comments are from student responses to the project, and I am grateful to the cohort of English 221-A students (Fall 2019 at Sacred Heart University), who were willing and generous participants in this assignment.

Figure 2 Annotating *A Midsummer Night's Dream* using the augmented reality application Thyng: images of fruit

figure out how to get students to read, it was interesting to recognise in my students' responses a desire for something 'other than reading'. One student articulated the theory that students' cognitive processes are changing: 'I think AR should be used more often. The world is changing and so are our minds. It's time literature does the same.'

In the limited time we worked on this app/augmented annotation, students had varying degrees of success. They all felt they could have benefited from more time and a greater number of assets. Still, some were able to point to rich possibilities. Figure 3 shows how the flood and fire in the first fairies' entrance can be depicted to demonstrate the impact of climate and natural disasters on human beings which the play points to, and which deepened the student's interpretation of Titania and Oberon's fight. In Video 1, a student created a forest on her desk and included Vivien Leigh's Titania. In this video, we can see what the student described about her experience with the technology: 'It definitely caused me to think about how someone would bring this to life on a stage. It posed questions such as, "How would the actors portray the emotions behind their characters' feelings?" and "What parts (if need be) would a director cut out?"' I found this response, and others along similar lines, extremely encouraging.

Although the restrictions of time and resources did not allow for a trip to the theatre, I was able to use smartphone technology – often disparaged as antithetical to serious literary study – to foreground the theatrical dimension implicit in Shakespearean drama. The interactive, immersive capabilities of AR can draw students into thinking about the physicality and materiality of performance in a way that is adjacent to the specialised skills of the director, costume designer, set designer, actors, and others. In so doing, it draws on the unique cognitive skills of twenty-first-century readers in order to address the challenges of the twenty-first-century classroom. While these experiments may not constitute a comprehensive solution to the range of hurdles that technology presents for today's instructors, I contend that they are nevertheless worthy of careful consideration because they underline the value of engaging students on their own terms, and because they point a way forward for Shakespeare instructors looking for practical ways to leverage technological assets.

Figure 3 Annotating *A Midsummer Night's Dream* using the augmented reality application Thyng: images of floods and fire

Video 1 Annotating *A Midsummer Night's Dream* using the augmented reality application Thyng: a student created a forest on her desk and included Vivien Leigh's Titania. Video available at www.cambridge.org/wittek-mcinnis.

5 Real Presence in the Virtual Classroom

Erin Sullivan

I am writing this section in the middle of 2020, several months into the worldwide coronavirus lockdowns. If we were all using our computers, phones, and tablets a lot already, then it goes without saying that we are using them even more now. Which makes me wonder: what does it mean to do something 'virtually' at this point in history, and where exactly is 'reality'? Of course, virtual reality (VR) as an industry is not only real but thriving, with the tools that it produces attempting to create feelings of embodied presence in a place different from the one in which the participant is physically located. As so many contributions to this collection attest, VR opens up new possibilities in the classroom, transporting students to places otherwise inaccessible. In this section, however, I want to think about virtual reality in a different way, decapitalising its key words and exploring what it means in a more general, even mundane sense. I want to ask whether our underlying assumptions about what constitutes 'virtual' as opposed to 'real' experience are changing as digital togetherness becomes an increasingly normal and even dominant feature in our lives, and what that might mean for all the college and university classrooms in the process of moving online.

In 2020, as every organisation that revolves around the principle of embodied togetherness is trying to figure out how to make what they do work in the digital sphere, questions about the relationship between the 'virtual' and the 'real' are reaching something of a tipping point – but they are by no means new. For nearly a decade, Nathan Jurgenson has been critiquing the concept of 'digital dualism', by which he means the 'fallacy of separate digital and physical spheres' (Jurgenson 2012: 88). '[T]echnology and society, the digital and the physical, media and humans, have imploded and augmented each other', Jurgenson writes. 'We cannot focus on one side, be it human or technology, without deeply acknowledging the other' (2012: 84). To suggest that what is online is always 'virtual' (and implicitly lesser) and what is offline is always 'real' (and implicitly better) is to insist on a categorical distinction that is increasingly impossible to sustain – and one that universities themselves are now eager to dispel as students request discounted fees for online-only instruction. For so many of us, online and offline life constantly intertwine, producing a mingled yarn, as someone might say, in which the good and the ill cannot be systematically ascribed.

This often chaotic interweaving of the 'virtual' and the 'real' has shaped my own teaching career, which over the past two decades has included as much instruction online as in person. Looking back, I am not entirely sure how this has happened: I am by no means an expert in digital technology, and my own education mostly took place in traditional, brick-and-mortar classrooms. I am also fortunate that I have not found myself forced into online teaching; it is a direction I have chosen willingly. Perhaps this is because I have never seen it as fundamentally, irredeemably different from the kind of teaching I do – and love to do – in more traditional settings. Through the years I have also learned about the advantages of online education, including more accessible classrooms, more diverse students, and, consequently, more encounters that challenge my own assumptions about our field and the best way to teach it. I have also learned a great deal about what real, meaningful presence looks and feels like in an online teaching space, and how it compares to that found in the physical classroom. There is a lot, I will suggest, that is intrinsically shared; it is in the extrinsic contexts that the real difference lies.

In our culture, there is a lot of talk about being 'present' – about 'showing up' and making people 'feel seen'. In many ways, such language represents a thinned-out take on philosophies of mindfulness – 'McMindfulness', as Ronald Purser has dubbed it – and any articulation along these lines understandably courts suspicion (Purser 2019). And yet, being present in a committed, relaxed, responsive, and absorbed way has been the skill that has helped me most in the online classroom. While it is impossible – and misguided – to generalise too much about distance-learning students, one thing that consistently comes up in feedback is a desire for community, interaction, immediacy, and a sense of belonging. Unsurprisingly, our students like to feel like their instructors care about them and that they have a relationship with us, and they get frustrated if they feel like they are being treated impersonally or as a second thought. This no doubt sounds familiar to all educators, whether they work online or in person, because these desires reflect pedagogical values that are fundamental to all good educational experiences. Students want their instructors to be present, in a cognitive and emotional way, and to relate to them as individuals who are striving to learn and grow.

It is this principle that leads me to suggest that creating a feeling of real presence is the most important thing that an instructor brings, alongside subject knowledge, to any online classroom. Once again, such an argument is by no means new; in fact, it reiterates one of the oldest pedagogical tenets of distance-learning education. Nearly half a century ago, Michael G. Moore laid the groundwork for his theory of 'transactional distance', by which he meant the 'distance of understandings and perceptions, caused in part by the geographic distance, that has to be overcome by teachers, learners and educational organizations if effective, deliberate, planned learning is to occur' (Moore 1991: 2; see also Moore 1972). To a certain extent, this theory articulated what was obvious: when students and teachers do not share the same physical space, cognitive and emotional distance widens, and work must be done to bridge it.

But notice that Moore describes such distance as caused 'in part' by geography, a phrasing that hints at the fact that putting everyone back in the same place would not necessarily solve the problem. Indeed, he goes on to suggest that 'In any educational programme there is *some* transactional distance, even where learners and instructors meet face to face' (Moore 1991: 3). This is because transactional distance, at its core, is not about physical geography or proximity, but about the experience of cognitive and emotional connection. Although distance-learning settings tend to involve greater transactional distance, due to the inherent challenges posed by not being together in the same room, it is entirely possible for an on-site, in-person class to have more transactional distance than a well-taught online one. As everyone knows, being physically present and together in a classroom comes with no guarantee that everyone will feel committed, involved, valued, and engrossed in the educational experience at hand. If an instructor does not make herself present and alert to her students in a meaningful way, it does not matter if they are sharing the same physical space. They are still distant.

So how do we create a feeling of real, committed presence in the online classroom, and in doing so minimise the transactional distance that shapes this supposedly virtual environment? I could suggest many novel possibilities, including the use of virtual reality technologies that might place instructors and students in the same digital room. More than a decade ago, several universities bought 'land' and set up learning spaces in Second Life, an online world where participants could (and in fact still can) interact as avatars in a variety of ways (Lagorio 2007). More recently, teachers around the world have used video games like *Minecraft* and *Animal Crossing* to stage online graduation ceremonies for their students (Groux 2020). It is not too far of a stretch to imagine three-dimensional, virtual reality classrooms, powered by Oculus or Vive headsets, that might allow students and teachers to experience one another's presence in an embodied, proprioceptive way. But as exciting as this would be, it is by no means essential for meaningful learning, and at least for the time being the barriers to realisation would almost certainly increase feelings of frustrated disconnection for many students. As far as VR technologies have come in the past ten years, they have still not gone mainstream, meaning that cost, lack of technical know-how, and feelings of self-consciousness inevitably get in the way of day-to-day classroom use.

Instead, the 'technologies' I find most effective in online teaching are the most basic, mundane, and accessible ones – the ones that barely even register as technologies in a glamorous, futuristic sense to students anymore. Asynchronous discussion boards, informal, self-made videos, one-to-one phone calls, and, yes, email: these are the staples of the online classrooms I have taught in, which have included students from a wide range of educational backgrounds, geographical settings, and ages (only a minority of those I have taught would identify as digital natives). For me, the most crucial features of these technologies are their ease of access for as diverse a group of students as possible and the responsiveness with which I as an instructor can use them. With these two factors in place, my students can engage regularly and straightforwardly in our class, and I can meet their efforts in a swift and supportive manner. That two-way, iterative form of exchange, strengthened by genuine commitment to one another and the mutual respect it brings, is what creates a sense of real, shared presence in the online classroom, even if we never occupy same physical space or even the same time.

It is for these reasons that, until very recently, I would not have included group videoconferencing in my list of everyday digital teaching tools. Although I have held optional videoconferences in all my distance-learning classes for several years, I have found that the take-up has been low (usually about 20 per cent of the cohort). This is no reason to discontinue them, of course: among the students who do come, the feedback has always been positive, with participants regularly saying how valuable, involving, and even immersive they find the experience of interacting with their instructors and peers in real time. The fact that we have never gotten anything close to a majority for such sessions, however, has indicated two things to me about our students, who are typically several years out of their BA and have jobs and families that their studies must fit around. First, participating in synchronous sessions just isn't realistic for those with very busy lives which stretch across a number of time zones, and second, group videoconferencing hasn't been familiar and mainstream enough for the majority of our students to be able to incorporate it into their studies in a low-key, low-stress way.

All that has changed, of course, within months. Over April 2020, global use of the videoconferencing software Zoom increased thirtyfold, with its membership rising to 13 million in the UK alone (Sherman 2020; 'UK's Internet Use' 2020). The result, according to Ofcom, the UK's communications regulator, has been a 'radical change' in 'online behaviour', both nationally and around the world ('UK's Internet Use' 2020). With this dramatic shift have come new opportunities for creating the experience of shared presence – a kind of virtual reality, I would suggest – in the online classroom. Although the rapid rise of videoconferencing does not erase the first obstacle to participation that I mentioned – busy lives in sometimes vastly different time zones – it does mean that more of our students are using it on a regular basis for many different purposes, and accordingly that they're more comfortable with incorporating it into their studies.

This increased familiarity also means greater awareness of the different ways videoconferencing can be used. Although everyone interacting with their cameras and microphones on, talking enthusiastically to one another in real time, might seem like the ideal way of participating, it is not feasible for all our students. Again, practical constraints like work commitments, caring responsibilities, and digital connectivity can all get in the way of taking part in this fashion. But, as we are all quickly learning, there are different ways to be present in a Zoom call, and the ability to have one's microphone and/or camera off and to participate by listening in while doing other things significantly increases what we are able to do alongside our daily duties. This is why, when I start teaching again in a few months, videoconferencing will feature much more prominently in my efforts to create real presence in the online classroom. I still won't be making participation mandatory, though I'm sure that many others will, especially if they are teaching undergraduates who would otherwise be arriving on campus for in-person classes.

Of course, a tool like Zoom or Microsoft Teams is no magic wand for creating feelings of shared experience and presence: after just a few months of using them round the clock, many of us are already all too aware of their shortcomings, including the fatigue they can induce and the stilted conversations they often create. As one journalist jokingly put it, too much Zooming can leave a person 'feel[ing] like an emotionally bereft alien struggling to comprehend the mysteries of human connection' (Cauterucci 2020). And yet, having taught for many years in mostly asynchronous online classrooms, I have found that there is something particularly productive and bonding about sharing the same time as a group, even if the chosen 'place' leaves something to be desired and the appointed hour can feel very different depending on one's time zone. This is especially true for open-ended, seminar-style discussions, where learning is more about listening and responding, and then listening and responding again, than it is about the presentation of rehearsed knowledge. Perhaps in the future, higher-spec digital spaces will allow students to come together in a more embodied, intimate, and less emotionally alien way. But for now, the enormous pedagogical importance of ease of use and accessibility means low-fi videoconferencing and the possibilities of presence it enables are the VR tools that have truly come of age in this historic moment.

That said, I want to go back to the question – and for many, the problem – of what kinds of engagement these synchronous technologies enable, and what we are learning about ourselves and the nature of presence as we use them. As I mentioned, as videoconferencing has gone mainstream, we have not only discovered ways in which we can use it to participate in new activities online, but also how we can do so alongside all the other tasks that demand our attention at home. I am sure I am not the only person who has listened in on a videoconference while looking after children, writing emails, or making lunch or dinner, perhaps typing the occasional comment into the chat. Indeed, over the past few months, media outlets have delighted in covering the biggest faux pas of the Zoom era, including woeful cases of people accidentally leaving their video on while using the bathroom or even taking a shower in front of their classmates and colleagues. Such stories serve as cautionary tales to us all as we incrementally push the limits of what and how much can be done while tending to activities that, if carried out in person, would typically demand the outward performance of full attentiveness, if not the inward reality of it.

But what interests me even more than the evolving social etiquette surrounding the use of videoconferencing is the kind of experience we and our students derive through these technologies as we weave them more and more into other day-to-day activities. As the 'virtual' and the 'real' become less about one or the other and more about both at the same time, our lives are at once 'augmented', as Jurgenson puts it (2012), while also pulled in many directions. The idea of the 'attention economy', in which the 'scarce resource' of human attention becomes increasingly precious in a world of 'information competition', has been around since at least the start of the twenty-first century (Davenport and Beck 2001: 9, 20). I would argue, however, that it is entering a new phase as many people rapidly adjust to layering work, family life, studying, managing a household, keeping in touch with loved ones, and many other activities onto one another more or less at once.

Although life in lockdown has physically and geographically become very bounded, for many it has never been more experientially fluid. The divisions between different aspects of life, both online and off, have become thoroughly blurred, as children run into the frames of video calls, deliveries arrive during work meetings, emails ping in the middle of homeschool sessions or family Zoom quizzes, and enticing digital events hosted around the world take place throughout the day and night. It is telling that during the pandemic so many articles have focused on the concept of 'mental bandwidth', or 'the limited store of focused attention we have to expend in any one day' (Wallace and Patrick 2020). This cognitive, emotional, and indeed physical entity becomes even more precious, and therefore strained, 'when we are navigating unfamiliar territory' – such as life during unprecedented times (Wallace and Patrick 2020).

But what does all this mean for teaching and for the online classrooms so many of us are busy creating? Those reading this section, some months or even years after it was written, will know better than me right now. But based on my experiences teaching in March and April 2020, and working remotely through the next several months and counting, my guess would be that the importance of cultivating real, focused presence will become ever greater, even as the practical challenges of doing so will mount. With both students and teachers distracted and spread thin, connecting with one another online and shutting out the noise of the world (and our households) will be both urgent and potentially unachievable.

As we meet in real time with our students through Zoom or Teams or whatever else, we will know that they are at once engaging with us and managing their own complicated, multitasking lives. Even before the pandemic, my distance-learning students told me that they listened to lecture recordings while driving to work or watched teaching videos at 1.5x speed. This does not bother me: it seems canny, and indeed conscientious – how many lectures have traditional, on-site students simply skipped? But it also suggests that undivided attention is not something we can expect from our students, or perhaps ourselves, as we move into this brave new world of widespread online teaching. Focus, and the feelings of immersion and presence it brings, will be an increasingly scarce commodity in our classrooms, as they will be almost everywhere else.

This is, perhaps, where higher-tech, more physically immersive forms of VR could really thrive, were financial barriers, digital know-how, and bandwidth of both the human and non-human variety no longer issues. Even more valuable than the proprioceptive qualities of embodiment that it offers, I think, are the experiential boundaries between 'here' and 'there' that it creates. One of the biggest critiques of VR equipment has been the way it requires users to don clunky headsets and cut themselves off from everyday life. Participants 'can't play on the go', and this single fact makes VR 'a fundamentally different beast' from the vast majority of technologies that we use regularly and seamlessly in our lives (Spaull 2019). But perhaps the previously invisible advantages of such a quality are now becoming apparent: having a technology that can take us out of the flow of daily life, and cut us off from the literal and metaphorical noise that continuously invades our work-home-study-social space, is no bad thing. Liam Jarvis has argued that the 'ontological and relational desire that undergirds much immersive experience' – and VR experience in particular – 'is to *feel more fully with the body of another*', and in doing so to at last '*become the other body*' (2019: 3–4). I wonder, though, if at this point in history that 'other' is less the embodied identity of someone else, and more a parallel version of our own selves, projected into a world else-where – one of both physical togetherness, and of quiet, absorbing focus.

And yet we do live in a world in which cost, IT savvy, digital infra-structure, and the many and immediate demands of daily life shape our existence. For me, this means the best we can do is to make the most of the more mundane, accessible, and less bounded 'VR' tools we have, and to practice ways in which we can be as present as possible through them. With the classroom less circumscribed than ever, it will at once be more accessible and convenient, and more vulnerable to thin, wandering forms of attention. Being there for each other will require more focus than ever, but I do believe that, with effort, conscientious respect for one another, and some trial and error, we will find ways to make it possible. If we manage to get it right, the result will be something very real, and perhaps even the thing that finally helps us take the 'virtual' out of how we think about life online.

III Current Projects and Future Directions

6 Infinite Space:
Notes towards Shakespeare's Virtual Reality Future
Michael Ullyot

A few months into the coronavirus pandemic, Fareed Zakaria's book *Ten Lessons for a Post-pandemic World* posited that comparatively competent Northern European governments offered Americans 'a path to a new world' of market efficiency tempered by social democracy (Joffe 2020). Predictions are a dangerous gambit, particularly those from the midst of disruptive change – dangerous because the inevitable next disruption undermines and obviates them. This section is about global media but takes lessons from and is informed by the global pandemic of 2020. Writing from its midst, as media and theatre companies adapt their revenue models, I look back to past virtual reality (VR) Shakespeare adaptations to assess their limitations in order to predict their future. Emerging technologies and asynchronous, distributed media platforms will influence production designs, while teaching and delighting.

There are many categories of VR experiences. We can plot them on a spectrum between imaginary and real.

- At the imaginary end are worlds existing only as digital renderings, comparable to those in video games or animated films. Typically, the player or audience can move freely in these worlds, examining and interacting with 3D digital objects (things and characters) from multiple positions and orientations.
- At the real end of the spectrum are physical spaces captured with multi-directional cameras, appearing more or less as they do in the real world. The viewer's position is restricted by camera placement(s), and our views of spaces, actors, and properties are limited to the sides that are oriented towards our position(s).
- Between these two extremes is the range of compound environments and objects: real actors in virtual spaces, for instance, or virtual properties in real spaces. Nearer the centre of the spectrum are environments that mix

real with virtual features and properties, and real actors with virtual ones. (On 'the relationship between the virtual and the real', see Erin Sullivan's section (Section 5) in this Element).

The five past Shakespeare VR adaptations I examine in this section are situated on the real end of this spectrum: live actors perform in more or less real environments with varying degrees of digital graphics. All five are live-action VR performances of excerpted or abridged Shakespeare plays that fix the viewer's position to a stationary or moving 360-degree camera, with greater or lesser success meeting three criteria: seamless mixing of real and virtual elements; smooth transitions between camera positions and edits; and unforced, natural inducements to orient viewers towards the principal action.

Past

King of Infinite Space (2017) is an early, experimental project mounted by the immersive theatre company Roll the Bones to promote a feature-length film captured on the grounds of a castle in Tipperary. Heavily laden with digital enhancements, it reveals the drawbacks of shifting the viewer's position with jarringly disorienting transitions between locations in the midst of Hamlet's speech about losing his mirth. Shifting abruptly to a graveyard, we watch him rise from the ground into a sky full of stars, also falling upward. Actors in the play's closing sword fight walk right through the viewer, and the production feels both experimental and ill conceived. In the same year (2017), a company called Virtuality produced the *Shakesperiences* series, offered on the Samsung VR app, which seems to have stopped at a single brief video in which a holographic Lady Macbeth performs her 'unsex me here' speech amid a digitally rendered courtyard that looks distinctly unreal, while multiple contrails of spirits encircle her like Harry Potter's Dementors. These two projects offer lessons in production design such as camera placements, and post-production decisions such as edits and special effects.

Hamlet 360: Thy Father's Spirit (2019), produced by the Commonwealth Shakespeare Company in collaboration with Google and the VR company Sensorium, is a more polished, extended adaptation of *Hamlet* as an hour-long 360-degree film. Its setting is a derelict theatre, with paint peeling from fading pillars. Its action is limited to an open space perhaps thirty metres square, with an elevated stage spanning one side and an irregular platform the other. In this space are some large properties – a car, a four-poster bed, a bathtub, a large immersion tank – along with several chairs, Oriental carpets, and occasional tables topped with Art-Nouveau-esque lamps. Like the *King of Infinite Space*, there are transitions between the viewer's positions, typically between scenes but occasionally within them. *Hamlet 360*'s editors use fade-outs and -ins to smooth scene transitions, and to signal a shift of position using a ghostly swirling-smoke effect to surround the viewer, evoking the typical image of the Ghost on the foggy battlements of Elsinore. (The viewer is, throughout, cast in the disembodied role of King Hamlet's ghost.) There are also a few less graceful mid-scene shifts of position, including one in the final sword fight when Gertrude is mid-sentence; however, for the most part, the transitions are smooth and filmic. The two most striking mid-scene shifts of position are underwater, to join Hamlet in his suicide attempt in the midst of the 'To be or not to be' soliloquy; and to witness Ophelia's drowning from beneath her corpse. Other post-production techniques encourage viewers to look towards the performers rather than elsewhere: given our freedom to orient ourselves in any direction, this is a distinct problem for VR's designers. In *Hamlet 360*, momentous speeches like Claudius' confession soliloquy force our perspective with a red-shift and zooming effect added in post-production. It is powerfully suggestive, but not constraining: we need only to turn our heads to either side to see other set features distorted and curved which could have been darkened altogether. *Hamlet 360*, the most extensive and most polished of these five VR adaptations, suggested the three criteria I use to evaluate them – even if it fell short of meeting some of those criteria.

The last two adaptations I consider make direct use of theatrical settings, with varying results. The first is the American Shakespeare Center (ASC)'s 360-degree documentary introduction to their Blackfriars Playhouse in Staunton, Virginia – a replica of the London theatre for which Shakespeare wrote many plays. This is accompanied by two speeches from *Hamlet*, putting the viewer in the position of a spectator – though at stage centre, immediately downstage from the actors. Though this mildly awkward position is fixed, the films provide a sense of this theatre's proportions and sightlines. And they are vastly more successful at this than the Royal Shakespeare Company's brief film of Alex Hassell in his 2015 role as Henry V. As he delivers the St. Crispin's Day speech to an empty stage and stalls at the Royal Shakespeare Company's (RSC) Swan Theatre, the viewer hovers overhead at an unnatural height that no real-world audience would ever inhabit. In both productions, it would have been worthwhile to give viewers the option of sitting in the stalls or on a balcony – though multiple positions surrounding live performances would require post-production concealment of the other cameras.

Present

Time now to offer my promised notes towards future VR adaptations of Shakespeare's plays, based on the limitations and achievements of these past productions – and on the period of media disruption accelerated by the coronavirus pandemic beginning in early 2020. My argument now turns to the effects of closing live theatres and cinemas in response to that pandemic – namely, the shift among large media and theatre companies to online distribution for socially isolated audiences.

Facing sudden, sharp declines in revenue from live performances, which resumed only in October 2020, London's National Theatre (NT) released sixteen of its thirty NTLive productions, intended for cinema broadcast and paywalled streaming services, for free on YouTube from April to August 2020. 'Theatres around the world are closed and facing a devastating impact from Coronavirus,' they wrote on title cards before every production. 'Theatre and the arts are a positive force for our community in turbulent times,' said the next card. The NT's appeal came on the third: 'As you enjoy this recorded performance, please consider a donation to support this great industry.' Then came the text codes and numbers to donate ten or twenty pounds to the NT, and in one case (*A Streetcar Named Desire*) to their co-production company the Young Vic.

Long before the lockdown, the NT was among many theatre companies using cinema broadcasts to distribute recordings of live performances: over the past decade, the Metropolitan Opera, the Royal Shakespeare Company, the Old Vic, and others have exploited this additional revenue and their distribution stream, and in this era of streaming video, cinemas are glad to host their prestige products.[12] But the NT was the only company to do it so extensively for free; the RSC, the Globe, and others largely remained behind paywalls or proprietary services like 'Theatre in Video'.[13]

The pandemic has also seen large media companies like Disney adapt its distribution plans, though far more aggressively than the NT did. Normally films like its live-action adaptation of *Mulan* (2020) and its live recording of Broadway musical *Hamilton* (2020) would have appeared exclusively in cinemas before shifting to streaming platforms. But with the new Disney+ platform eager to compete with Netflix, Prime Video, and others in a crowded landscape, and the conglomerate compensating for lost revenue from in-person leisure and entertainment offerings, Disney released both films on Disney+ in the summer of 2020. This example illustrates the wider transition away from synchronous, collective, public performances towards asynchronous, atomised, private performances – a trend that began with the shift from cable TV to streaming services but had not meaningfully impacted the cinematic theatre broadcast before the pandemic.

There is little reason to believe that the incremental reopenings of theatres and resumptions of live performances will slake the media giants' or theatre companies' appetites for the revenue streams that asynchronous distribution offers. Why would they stop? Where money is to be made, productions will follow. Already these companies are leveraging distribution platforms that are agnostic about the device on which you watch them: YouTube videos play just as readily on phones and tablets as on desktops or laptops, to say nothing of televisions – indeed, the company reports that 70 per cent of its global 'watch time' is on mobile devices.[14] YouTube is also

---

[12] The first essay collection on this medium of Shakespeare performances is Aebischer et al. 2018.

[13] In September 2020, the Globe released one of its seventy-three productions to YouTube: *Romeo and Juliet* (2019), preceded by an appeal for donations. The RSC issued only a video appeal to 'Keep Your RSC Open for Everyone' in April 2020.

[14] www.youtube.com/intl/en-GB/about/press

on Oculus, a VR headset and media company owned by Facebook, which is how I viewed *Hamlet 360*. When these and future generations of headsets are as ubiquitous as today's tablets, surely YouTube VR will offer much more content. Someday, perhaps, the Netflix of VR will offer its subscribers VR films, both animated and live action, and media companies like Disney will vastly expand their VR productions. Shakespeare will then revert to the niche entertainment that he is in our present-day media environment saturated with superheroes. Only well-funded organisations like the RSC or the Globe Theatre will have the resources and experience to record live theatre for VR audiences, as they once did for cinema broadcast audiences.

Future

The Globe's considerable library of seventy-three filmed performances on their Globe Player (streaming) and Globe OnScreen (cinema broadcast) services are, like the ASC's Blackfriars VR project, quite firmly within Shakespeare's niche. They teach viewers about historical performance spaces, but both the ASC and the RSC suggest how the Globe might move past the conventional medium of multiple-perspective edited films to immerse viewers in its space. The Globe might follow their lead and capture performances on multiple 360-degree cameras (concealed in post-production), giving viewers the freedom to shift out vantage points from (say) the tiring-house balcony to the yard to the galleries to the stage itself. The result would be a far more expansive sense of performance constraints and conditions.

Shakespeare's niche, as suggested by the institutional subscription models for RSC and the Globe's recordings, is solidly educational – but not only for theatre historians. Performances are also a vital resource for teaching students to interpret Shakespeare's words, and it is conceivable that future VR adaptations could promote that interpretation (see for example Stephen Wittek's description of the *Shakespeare-VR* project in Section 8. Post-production design choices governing subtitles, glosses, summaries, patterns, and other language features and metadata could complement the recorded performance. My students are always turning on the captions when they watch a Shakespeare film or recorded performance so they can learn to read the language by seeing how an actor performs it. Curious about its effect in VR, I turned on the captions in *Hamlet 360* and found them obtruding awkwardly into my field of view; they ought to have been like the surtitles in foreign-language opera. The text, in other words, felt like an afterthought, like captions.

What if, instead, the actors' words were integrated more deliberately, making overt design choices to highlight its adaptations of text to speech? What if, for instance, the words unfurled on a scrolling display timed to coincide with the audible speech? I am speculating about such interfaces because of how the designers of *Hamlet 360* integrate the end credits. In lieu of a linear flow, the credits accumulate in a spatial array beginning with the cast list in the centre of the visual field and radiating outward in both the leftward and rightward directions. They fade in gradually and sequentially, prompting me to recognise that text in VR can appear wherever and whenever it suits the performance. We are so accustomed to watching credits roll steadily upward that when an innovative designer departs from such conventions it has the effect of a shock.

What, then, might a future VR post-production designer do with Shakespeare's texts? I have already suggested how they could complement and illustrate the actors' words, with due care for timing and for placement. But I imagine a textual layer overtop rhetorical figures – like the *stichomythia* that characterises Richard of Gloucester's wooing of Lady Anne in *Richard III* (1.2), say, or the multivariate figures that propagate through Berowne's wordplay in *Love's Labour's Lost*. Here we are moving beyond operatic surtitles to a kind of verbally augmented reality, which might even overlay images of people, places, or things mentioned in passing but not (virtually) present. The potential to overwhelm the viewer's senses is acute, and the interpretive decisions to fixate on one facet of language over another would need to be flexible; I can imagine, for instance, giving viewers the ability to set preferences to text features of interest: scene and character summaries for the first-time viewer, figures of speech for the linguistically curious, and visual annotations or glosses for the social historians. There are various possibilities for bringing supplementary, illustrative, explanatory, and other editorial material into the audience's sensory field, after user experience studies and other deliberations. My suggestions make a leap from *Hamlet 360*'s subtitles, credits, act numbers, and other textual over-lays – a leap, that is, from minimal to maximal, that may never come to pass.

Of these two future scenarios I have offered, the multi-camera theatre recordings and the text augmentations, little more is required than the willingness of production designers and the wizardry of post-production designers. Now for a final prediction that requires some technological advances. A limitation of present-day VR that will someday seem quaint is its restriction of the viewer to one (camera) position relative to the action. Motion capture and three-dimensional scanning technologies will advance sufficiently to obviate the fixed positions of today's 360-degree VR cameras, whose only advantage over conventional digital cameras is their multi-directionality. Replacing those cameras with a set of 3D scanners positioned around the periphery of a live-action performance will capture enough data to recreate and render multidirectional images of moving, emoting, speak-ing, live actors from every conceivable vantage. Why? To free the audience from our fixed position, giving us the ability to wander as freely through live-action scenes as through computer-generated scenes.

The implications of this forecasted future are that VR games and VR performances will merge their immersive capabilities, and we will be able to wander freely through performances' rendered bodies and spaces. From there it is easy to imagine locative markers embedded through the rendered space, permitting an audience member (one headset at a time) to move fluidly through this space, triggering new adjacent performances: so while Hamlet is lugging Polonius' guts to the neighbour room, for instance, Claudius is readying a search party for the corpse. The resulting multi-plicity and simultaneity of performances will do violence to narrative chronology, but no more than a non-linear spatial theatre performance does. The Shakespearean example that comes readily to mind is Punchdrunk Theatre's *Sleep No More*, an adaptation of *Macbeth* that fractures the play's narrative sequence into vignettes, interactions, speeches, properties, places, and scenes unfolding simultaneously in the various spaces of a five-floor warehouse recreated as the McKitterick Hotel, through whose hundred rooms the audience wanders at will. Felix Barrett, one of its directors and designers, claims that there is no one way to 'experience' *Sleep No More*: 'Some people choose to explore the space methodically, while others follow actors. Some people treat it as theatre, others as an art installation. There's no one right way to do it.'[15] It thus translates the experience of reading *Macbeth* into apprehending the play materially as well as spatially. As William Worthen comments, 'the audience enters the space rather than observing it', and 'each spectator's progress creates a poetic, associative narrative' (2012: 82). The ability to thus engage directly and freely in space and with things does allow each spectator to create their own interpretation of *Sleep No More*, and of *Macbeth* itself.

Punchdrunk's highly successful production in New York is on hiatus due to the pandemic, but in 2016 the company launched a satellite production in Shanghai. China is thus the next node in the global culture network to localise an American production of an English play about a Scottish tyrant. As local theatres close and people retreat from one another into atomised, sanitary replicas of collective culture, VR may represent a pathway to the brave new post-pandemic world that we will regret. Yet if the National Theatre foretold correctly that theatre can be 'a positive force for our community', then Shakespeare may do more good than harm.

---

[15] *Sleep No More* playbill, 29.

7 *'Death or Punishment by the Hands of Others':*
Presence, Absence, and Virtual Reality in Red Bull Theater's
The White Devil *(2019)*
Jennifer A. Low[16]

> And as imagination bodies forth
> The forms of things unknown, the poet's pen
> Turns them to shapes, and gives to airy nothing
> A local habitation and a name.
>
> *A Midsummer Night's Dream*, 5.1.14–17

> Only the poet, disdaining to be tied to any such subjection,
> lifted up with the vigor of his own invention, doth grow in
> effect another nature in making things either better than
> nature bringeth forth, or quite anew, forms such as never
> were in nature.
>
> Sir Philip Sidney, 'An Apology for Poetry,' 14

Like so many plays by Shakespeare and his contemporaries, John Webster's 1612 tragedy *The White Devil* literalises the common dramatic theme that links vision and surveillance. Louisa Proske, who directed the 2019 Red Bull Theater production at the Lucille Lortel Theatre, has observed that *The White Devil* is 'deeply a piece about power – power linked to seeing' (Proske 2020).[17] For that reason, when Proske directed the play, she drew upon the visual language of surveillance through the use of a variety of technological devices. In the play's climax, where Webster wrote an inset

---

[16] I'd like to express my gratitude to the Red Bull Theater's director of *The White Devil*, Louisa Proske, who graciously allowed me to interview her; to Anthony Guneratne, whose generous comments clarified my understanding of Jean Baudrillard's work; and to David McInnis and Lisa Starks, whose thought-provoking observations on this section have been helpful.

[17] In this instance as in several others, the production thematised an element already present in the play. See Farrah Lehman Den's (2011) treatment of the priority of sight over the other senses.

performance of a stylised battle, a 'fight at barriers,' Proske modernised the inset scene by making it a VR war game in acknowledgement of the popular tropes so notable in this play. In Proske's use of virtual reality, VR was not an audience experience but a spectacle seen from the outside. This use challenged spectators to rethink the primacy of vision and its purported link to power, a link that was heretofore upheld throughout the production.

When post-structuralists revisit Shakespeare and Sidney's conception of art as creation, they suggest that we should see the representational arts not as creators of worlds but as agents of reproduction. Baudrillard asserts that 'the false' is born in the Renaissance, that 'in the prowesses of stucco and baroque art . . . you read the metaphysic of the counterfeit' (1983: 87). The divide perceived between art and sincerity (a concern expressed frequently in Protestant culture from the early modern period to at least the early twentieth century) resembles the gap between sign and referent that only widens when more reproducible art forms arise: 'all the forms change once they are . . . *conceived from the point-of-view of their very reproducibility*, diffracted from a generating nucleus we call the model . . . Only affiliation to the model makes sense, and nothing flows any longer according to its end, but proceeds from the model, the "signifier of reference"' (Baudrillard 1983: 100–1).

Reproducibility is of course a recurrent concern in defining the nature of the arts, as is the aesthetic object's relation to a model. The issue is an important one in film studies; Christian Metz characterises the genre of film with a mixture of admiration and doubt:

> The unique position of the cinema lies in [the] dual character of its signifier: unaccustomed perceptual wealth, but at the same time stamped with unreality to an unusual degree. . . .
> The cinema involves us in the imaginary: it drums up all perception, but to switch it immediately over into its own absence, which is nonetheless the only signifier present.
>
> (1975: 45)

He asserts that the medium of film expands the power inherent in language: while a word may be the sign of an object, an image can serve as a synecdochic sign of an entire world. And when the medium is film, the image is a simulacrum, the ungraspable signifier of the thing.

In treating virtual reality, one must go a step farther. Virtual reality, 'technology that relies on software, hardware, and content but without the physical world and . . . 100% imaginary or synthetic' (Lion-Bailey and Lubinsky, 2020: xix) results from the generation of 'a real without origin or reality: a hyperreal' (Baudrillard 1996: 1). Its distance from reality, its manipulability renders it a product 'of imagination all compact' (*MND*, 5.1.8). In its commonest and most popular forms, it emphasises the visual in excess of the other senses and challenges our reliance on proprioception and the haptic as means of gathering information about our surroundings.

The repeated use of simulacra in Red Bull Theater's production of Webster's *The White Devil* was capped by the introduction of VR technology as props in the climax of the play. I view these reproductive techniques as a way of thematising the play of presence and absence in the play, a sophisticated riff on how power functions in *The White Devil* – most effective when its source is not present. In the Red Bull's production, the play, a mad chess game, showed power receding further and further from the stage until even the simulacrum of a video projection stood in for a power not visible on any platform, yet evident from prior manipulation. The Oculus Rift casques (or helmets) of Act Five, Scene Three helped to emphasise the isolation that results from distrust and acquiescence to treachery. The fantasy provided by VR substituted neatly for Webster's original staging of a fight at barriers, a nostalgic gesture towards a lost chivalric age. The result for the audience at *The White Devil* was the sight of the characters blindly swatting at illusory attackers, most of them completely unaware that danger was coming from an entirely different direction – the casques themselves.

Throughout *The White Devil*, characters attack one another most successfully at a distance. They act through agents or through the early modern equivalents of time bombs. Yet, through a network of intelligencers and conjurers, the powerful maintain their knowledge and even their sight of those they control. They are most dangerous when they are absent because it is then that their emissaries act on their behalf. Presence is less powerful – less hegemonic and less panoptic – than the lack of presence; seeing yields the most insight when it is achieved in absentia through the use of tools.

The Red Bull production linked absence and panoptic power by using simulacra (literally projections and videos) to represent spaces and people physically distant from Rome, the place the stage represents. The play begins with Count Lodovico discussing his banishment from Rome with two friends. In contrast to the original staging, in which Lodovico converses with two sycophants present at the decree, this production staged the conversation as a FaceTime session with Lodovico's face projected ten feet high. (The projection screen was part of the set, a glass-framed enclosure that sat like a tiring-house on a platform at the back of the stage.) Thus, Lodovico appeared as an image that the two actors onstage addressed, turning their backs on the audience.

The video of the Count was staged as an image of absence, already at a distance from Rome (i.e. the stage) and presumably stranded, away from his avenues of power, possibly for the entirety of the action. The first word, 'Banish'd?', made clear not only that he was away from Rome, but also that the sentence passed upon him prevented him from returning. Yet his absence did not prevent the force of his personality from coming across as a quasi-presence. The basic filmic technique of the close-up rendered him larger than life, in direct contrast to the actors onstage, who were turned to face the projection. The size of it dwarfed his informants, and the power of his age and vice were evident in the moving image. His shoulder-length grey hair curved around his face, and his muscular neck indicated a powerful body that, significantly, was not visible. His broad wrinkles and his threatening shout made his murderous character clear as he refuted the justice of the sentence: 'Fortune's a right whore,' he thundered (*The White Devil*, 1.1.4). The staging contrasted the physical presence of the two sycophants on the stage, standing downstage in the generic conventions of theatrical performance, with the video's close-up of Lodovico's face and shoulders, using the close-up as a standard camera technique for achieving intimacy and creating an impression of presence. The face that hovered above the heads of the sycophants and the booming sound of his transmitted voice both contributed to Lodovico's overmastering of the two men. Their comments were overruled and mocked by this powerful, vice-ridden character, who looked down on the live actors literally and figuratively and belittled them with his words and his contemptuous tone of voice.

The irony of his absence was particularly marked in his statement,

> Leave your painted comforts.
> I'll make Italian cut-works in their guts
> If ever I return. (1.1.50–2)

The statement contrasts the 'painted' or false comfort of his cohorts (still present in Rome) as a representation notable for its lack of reality, its lack of any true contact point with actual experience, compared with his pledge to make 'Italian cut-works', a graphic term for slicing into someone's intestines until they resemble lacy embroidery, as a revenge he will inflict upon his enemies in the future if his banishment is ever lifted so that his body can be present in Rome/onstage once again. While the threat is his attempt to override his absence, his inability to say 'when' (rather than '*if* I return') undermines the effect of his promise of future presence, reminding us that, though powerful, he can only depend on his own actions to achieve his revenge. Thus, his lack of presence, his inability to be onstage in 'Rome' save as an image, indicates a degree of powerlessness. Nonetheless, the close-up of Lodovico emphasises his ability physically to *over see* his sycophants, to look down upon them and perceive any prevarication or evasions they might attempt in order to avoid his ire. His appearance onscreen gave the impression that he had the capacity to control men even at a distance – and that his power would be exercised as effectively *in absentia* as if he were present.

For much of the play, the character who seems to be the most powerful is the Duke of Brachiano, who never appears onscreen. Present onstage almost constantly from 1.2, Brachiano seems able to command offstage events and even to gain the opportunity to watch them as 'visions'. Knowing that Vittoria Corombona, the woman he lusts after, refuses to commit adultery, he sends his retainers to kill off his own wife to clear a path for Vittoria. The scene of Duchess Isabella's death, described in the text as a dumb show, occurs in Red Bull's production as video projected onto the screen upstage. Brachiano confers with a conjurer who urges,

> Pray sit down,
> Put on this night-cap, sir, 'tis charm'd and now
> I'll show you by my strong-commanding art
> The circumstance that breaks your Duchess' heart. (2.2.20–3)

What followed appeared on the screen in black and white: a framed photo of Brachiano was visible on his duchess's dressing table, the lips smeared with some sticky substance. We, the spectators, watched voyeuristically with Brachiano as Isabella prepared for bed and kissed the photo, almost immediately dropping into a fit and dying, finally, as blood came out of her mouth. How many layers of reality are involved? In the video, Isabella kisses an image of her husband on which a real poison has been spread over the image of his lips; then she dies onscreen. She is not present on the stage – we watch the video of the scene just as Brachiano does with his back turned to the audience. The effect is ambiguous: we cannot be sure whether we are seeing a fantasy, a vision, or actual events. In contrast to the earlier use of the screen, this instance shows self-contained events in which the actors onstage are also mere spectators who do not interact or relate to what happens in the video. The only connection is, of course, is Brachiano's gaze, the sense of control conveyed by his calm observation of her enactment of hopeless love for him and her death, which results from his use of his knowledge of her habitual loving gesture. Proske asserts:

> At the heart of this society is this sick voyeurism. If Webster were writing the play today, he would be using videos. . . . For me the snuff film Brachiano commissions is ordered for his own visual pleasure. . . . Women in this world are always surveilled; men are always looking. (Proske 2020)[18]

Absence/distance is a form of safety for the powerful; if one commits treachery at a distance, one's responsibility cannot be traced.

---

[18] See also Katherine M. Carey's treatment of the dumb show as a moment when the audience experiences hypermediation, watching 'while at the same time observing Bracciano's reaction, two frames within one theatrical frame' (2007).

The video provides Brachiano with confirmation of his plot's success and the pleasure of power, the ability to watch Isabella's fate. It recalls the perspective glass used in such plays as *Friar Bacon and Friar Bungay*, *Macbeth*, and *The Travels of the Three English Brothers*, enabling panoptic control and serving as a tool that extends the physical body's power to manipulate (as the mage's books do in *Doctor Faustus* and *The Tempest*).[19] The video provides Brachiano with sight (presence) and safety (absence). It also highlights the eroticism of the voyeur, an element in early modern drama common in both tragedy (e.g. *Bussy D'Ambois*, *Othello*, *'Tis Pity She's a Whore*) and comedy (e.g. *Volpone*, *The Roaring Girl*, *Much Ado about Nothing*). Brachiano is unusual for his self-control even in the midst of his enjoyment of the erotic pleasures of observation.

The character who manifests the greatest understanding of the power of absence is the brother of the murdered Isabella: Francisco de Medici, Duke of Florence (renowned in seventeenth-century England as a wily intriguer). Francisco manifests a profound suspicion of signifiers: he inquires of Cardinal Monticelso about what Monticelso calls his 'black book', within which 'lurk / The names of many devils' (4.1.35–6). Noting that people with ready cash can bribe officials to have their names rased out of the list of intelligencers, murderers, and knaves, Francisco recognises 'the corrupted use some make of books' and, to shore up his spirits, conjures up the ghost of his dead sister, the Duchess Isabella, in an attempt to remember her vividly: 'Now I ha't – how strong / Imagination works! How she [Imagination] can frame / Things which are not! Methinks she [Isabella] stands afore me' (4.1.102–4).[20] Later in the play, he too manipulates the power of the written word by planting a letter that inspires Duke Brachiano to abscond with Vittoria Corombona, thereby running afoul of the law: 'How fortunate are my wishes. Why? 'Twas this / I only labour'd. I did send the letter / T'instruct him what to do. Thy fame, fond Duke, / I first have poison'd (4.3.52–5). Proske's staging of Francisco's manipulation of the newly made Pope Monticelso was, she says, inspired by an incident in

---

[19] Cf. McInnis 2013.

[20] Cf. Lord Kames' distinction, made in the eighteenth century, between 'real presence' and 'ideal presence' (Home 1765).

the movie *Wag the Dog* (1997): Francisco stands onstage, speaking into a cell phone; then the video screen shows the Pope reading a note passed to him with the words that Francisco uttered. He excommunicates Brachiano on the basis of his liaison with Vittoria, thus playing into Francisco's hands.

The final scene of Red Bull's production hammered home the point made throughout *The White Devil*: power is achieved through signifiers rather than the thing itself because signifiers can be manipulated in ways that presence cannot be. At a moment when villains and avengers seemed locked in a death embrace, a final projection appeared on the upstage structure: a close-up of Brachiano's frail and childish son, Giovanni, safely absent and much larger than life. From his vantage point he looked down upon the killers and inquired righteously, 'By what authority have you committed / This massacre?' (5.6.282–3). His indignation was shaken by Lodovico's outraged answer: 'By thine!', explaining that the boy's uncle, the Duke of Florence, compounded the plot. Though the dying villains were carted away by Giovanni's servants, the spectator's sense of justice is challenged by the truth in Lodovico's implication about who is responsible. The wheel has turned, and the Duke of Florence, no longer visible onstage, is running the show through an agent, his nephew. The deck will be cleared; it will superficially seem as though justice has been done, but in actuality, the game of power will simply have been won by the least visible player.

The audience of Red Bull Theater's *The White Devil* was inevitably implicated in the ubiquitous voyeurism throughout the play. Webster apportions guilt to all the characters who enjoy the pleasure and power of the gaze, and the spectators are no exception. The play's condemnation of the gaze gradually becomes stronger through all the inset performances and comes to a head with the showy game at barriers in which Brachiano is poisoned. This scene, which occurs in 5.3, is arguably the climax of the play – the first of several scenes in which villains meet their deaths. Shortly before the fight, Count Lodovico sprinkles the Duke of Brachiano's beaver with poison; then, in the midst of the fighting, Brachiano suddenly reels, shouting, 'Tear off my beaver . . . O my brain's on fire' (5.3.3–4). In early modern productions, the scene was undoubtedly the most spectacular incident in the play, with five of the main characters dressed in armour, engaging in a ceremonious war game. In Red Bull Theater's modern-dress production, a virtual war game is substituted for the fight at barriers, and the actors wear VR casques rather than helmets. This decision makes it possible to duplicate the precise means of poisoning Brachiano; yet, rather than staging a showy spectacle, spectacle is emptied out. Instead of a brave show of men in armour, spectators at the Red Bull production only saw the five characters wearing the casques, manipulating electronics, ducking and weaving aimlessly in the manner of people engaged in VR games. Their power, their skill in VR contrasted with their clueless appearance and their vulnerability to the hazards of reality.

The actors' use of Oculus Rift casques heightened the ludic nature of the fight at barriers and emptied out its violence even further. These luxury items of the early twenty-first century substitute for the costly parade armour of the courtly fight at barriers, which had already become a rare and nostalgic phenomenon by the time of the play's first performance in 1612. Significantly, the fight at barriers was no longer as closely linked with war even as early as the fifteenth century. Keen writes,

> Steadily, these sports were becoming more and more divorced from the central activity with which they were originally associated, real fighting in real war. Technical improvements and safety precautions, by reducing the danger of tourneying, reduced the resemblance with real battle. Important among these innovations was the tilt, the barrier dividing the lists which made it impossible for the horses of the combatants to collide accidentally; in engagement on foot the barrier across which the combatants struck at each other was a parallel innovation (1984: 205).

The sport is thus a recreation, not an actual expression of violence. It is, in fact, a reproduction, a signifier of the more-difficult-to-construct signified thing that is 'war' (or perhaps 'battle', an experiential synecdoche for 'war'). Virtual reality games carry both the recreational and the reproductive aspects of war games farther. The spectacle the scene provided in *The White Devil* reinforced the valorisation of strategy within the court intrigues and the audience's need to recognise their limited ability to assess the most skilful intriguer.

The significance of Webster's inset performance of sportive contest depends upon the spectators knowing the rules of the game. Like the wrestling match in *As You Like It*, *The White Devil*'s fight at barriers was not pure spectacle, nor was it a mêlée: it 'interrogates the boundaries of its own game and of social codes more generally ... Violence can be represented or "played"' (Marshall 1993: 266–7). The fight at barriers superficially resembles the fencing match in *Hamlet* in terms of the tension it produces between combat as sport and combat as 'demonstrative violence', a tension that hinges on the possibility that the combat 'might inflict real damage not in spite of but because of its vulnerability to being faked; it is not securely fixed in either a mimetic or a ludic realm' (Marshall 1993: 278, 276). But Webster's manipulation of this scene at barriers also diverges from the fencing exhibition in *Hamlet*: the poisoned foil must be used skilfully by a fencer in order for the poison to reach its intended mark, but the poison placed in Brachiano's helmet reverses its purpose: rather than protecting him, it kills him. In other words, Brachiano's poisoning has nothing to do with the game at barriers; the helmet is a prop emptied of its meaning as a tool of war. (The metonymic prop of the VR casque is distanced even further from war.) The other characters' fighting skills are irrelevant to the success of the plot.

Brachiano's response to the poison cuts short the ludic event and truncates the dramatic build-up of the staged sport. This interruption of a subplot's dramatic arc echoes a similar one earlier in the play: directly after Marcello formally challenges his brother Flamineo to a duel, the two brothers encounter one another unexpectedly and Flamineo casually runs Marcello through with his own sword. In both cases, a plot line that Webster sets in motion is abruptly ended or redirected towards another goal. The result is that the tension is lost and the audience's attention is brought up short.

Significantly, with Proske's substitution of VR casques, the spectators are excluded from the spectacle. Instead of becoming engaged by the combat, they see the characters in a non-performative mode, unselfconsciously stumbling around, easy targets for anyone not involved. Wholly absorbed in an illusory world, they perform in the virtual world for one another but seem to ignore their physical appearance. The characters are present onstage, yet not present to us; the actors perform as non-performers.

In their use of VR headsets, the Red Bull Theater confounds the audience's expectation of presence as power and nudges the audience to recognise the insufficiency of sight as a means for judgement. With the use of VR headsets as a vehicle for murder, Brachiano is punished not merely for villainy, but also for voyeurism. As Proske explains, 'Initially . . . the poison in our production [devoured him] through the eyes [alluding to] the sin of illicit viewing' (Proske 2020). Webster's play demonstrates the author's deep suspicion of sight, of the ethics of seeing and judging. What spies and voyeurs do, spectators at the play do as well – participate in inappropriate seeing and enact the same judgements as *The White Devil*'s servants and hangers-on (Goldberg 1987: 70–1). Only during the fight at barriers was the audience divided from the enactors of the drama. It was then, when the characters entered their private worlds of virtual reality, that the spectators were left to watch them. The sight of them ceasing to perform freed the spectator to watch them engage with one another as they looked at a reality invisible to the audience and jockeyed for a non-existent position in an illusory world. The characters remained off guard, immersed in a singular world, a world that could not be shared with others. The scene is almost an antitheatrical warning. It demonstrates the insufficiency of vision and the playwright's distrust of spectacle. In pragmatic terms, distance and absence enable the powerful to achieve their goals. Characters who can exercise these as tools of power remain pure, clean. By the same logic, then, the spectators must take partial responsibility by acknowledging what their presence at the spectacle has brought them: contamination from the sights they have seen.

8 Spaces in Headsets and Heads Set in Spaces: Notes on the Shakespeare-VR Project

Stephen Wittek

As is often the case for entries in the Cambridge Elements series, the present Element offers a forward-looking view of a new area of scholarly interest just beginning to coalesce. In addition to articulating the parameters of an emergent discussion, scholarship of this sort also serves a historical function because, like baby photos or architectural blueprints, it shows what the object of discussion looked like before it grew into maturity. Oriented by these dual perspectives – looking forward, but also imagining how the present moment might appear from a retrospective point of view in the future – I have gathered thoughts and observations gleaned from my experience over the past three years as the director of the *Shakespeare-VR* project (www.shakespeare-vr.library.cmu .edu). In what follows, my aim is to develop a snapshot of sorts that captures the project, but also the medium of virtual reality itself, at a moment when everything is still fuzzy and new. In so doing, my first goal is to provide some food for thought to fellow travellers engaged in the task of producing and

Figure 1 Screen capture from *Shakespeare-VR* production of *Hamlet*, starring Zoe Speas. Blackfriars Playhouse, November 2018

theorising virtual reality media, especially in relation to Shakespearean drama and education. In addition, I also hope to leave a record for future reference (for myself as much as for anyone else) because I have a strong sense that my perspective on these issues will change rapidly in relation to technological, artistic, and scholarly innovation. What follows, then, is something like the journal of an explorer after a winter or two on a new frontier, a document that is equally uncertain and optimistic, soberly aware of future challenges, but also intoxicated by the allure of wide-open potential.

From the beginning, the *Shakespeare-VR* project has hinged on the contention that an ability to visualise the embodied, spatial aspects of early modern theatrical experience is crucially important to an understanding of Shakespearean drama – an insight that comes naturally to actors and theatregoers, but is not nearly as obvious to students working from a text in a classroom. Following from this basic premise, the project proposes to bridge the gap between text and experience by offering virtual reality as a second-best alternative to attendance at a live performance. Unlike a novel or a poem, a Shakespearean play entails an implicit assumption of a specific type of theatre and specific conditions of performance, including a bare stage, universal lighting, spectators on three sides, minimal props, and a lively, intimate atmosphere conducive to audience interactivity and collective imagining. For readers unaccustomed to these conditions, a text such as *Hamlet* or *Lear* can seem fragmentary or opaque – a recipe that only lists half the necessary ingredients. In order to understand *how to* understand Shakespeare, students must have some sense of the conditions he had in mind when he wrote his plays.

To introduce the basics of early modern theatrical experience, instructors regularly employ two-dimensional visual aids, such as PowerPoint slides and video clips of live performances. Although these supplements may go a long way towards clarifying some basic distinctions between drama and other forms of literature, they can ultimately only offer a very abstract representation of what the early modern theatre actually looked and felt like, and are therefore a limited tool for demonstrating the physical dynamics of theatrical experience. In my view, and in the view of many other instructors, nothing can compete with the excitement and educational benefit of attending a live performance. Of course, for the vast majority of instructors and students, a trip to the theatre is simply not an option – but with the rising availability of inexpensive, mass market headsets, the prospect of bringing a taste of theatrical magic into the classroom is now more feasible than ever.

As suggested by my focus on space, embodiment, and experience, the pedagogical intervention I have conceived derives from practical approaches to Shakespeare instruction pioneered by educators at the American Shakespeare Center, the Globe Theatre, and the Folger Institute (Banks 2014; Charlton 2012). Founded on a philosophy of 'learning by doing', these approaches endeavour to supplement the traditional lecture with activities such as acting, vocalising, improvising, and other forms of exploration that foster a more physical engagement with dramatic texts. On a similar note, the project also builds on educative experiments in disciplines such as medicine and engineering, where researchers have begun to establish a compelling evidentiary basis for the potential of active learning activities situated within virtual environments (Freeman et al. 2014; Prince 2004; Merchant et al. 2014; Nicholson et al. 2006).

Although some vague notions for how to combine Shakespeare with virtual reality had been brewing in the back of my mind for several years, plans for the project did not really begin to develop until 2017 – shortly after my arrival at Carnegie Mellon University (CMU) – when a colleague mentioned that students at the university's Entertainment Technology Center (ETC) were on the lookout for faculty collaborators with interesting ideas. As I began to consider the venture more seriously, it occurred to me that a virtual reality project would fit nicely with the scholarly work I had done on theatrical space and the media culture of early modern England. As an added benefit, I also sensed an opportunity to apply my experience in the digital humanities to an endeavour oriented towards education and an ethic of open access, which is where my heart has always been in terms of digital scholarship. A few months later, following the submission of a hastily conceived funding proposal, I became the recipient of a modest internal award designated for new efforts to promote technology-enhanced learning. Slowly but surely, my hastily conceived ideas began to move towards reality – and virtual reality.

Looking back, I realise the entire endeavour would have very likely resulted in catastrophe were it not for the benefit of my collaborators. As it turned out, the students in the ETC programme were not especially eager to work on an education project. For the most part, they make games, rather than documentary-style experiences, and they have to work within a very tight semester-based schedule that does not leave much time for the ongoing, multifaceted project I had envisioned. More importantly, virtual reality production is expensive. As the hard reality of production costs came into contact with my soft budget projections, it became increasingly apparent that the modest amount of funding I had received was not likely to go as far as I had hoped.

It was therefore a great stroke of luck when ETC instructor Ralph Vituccio put me in contact with his colleague and collaborator Jaehee Cho, a former music video director who had recently founded the virtual reality start-up Stitchbridge (now Orta Interactive Studio). In consonance with my own inclinations, Jaehee's work leverages the novelty of virtual reality to foster reflection and emotional engagement, aiming to push the medium towards greater thoughtfulness and meaningfulness. For example, in *Injustice* (2015), he explores issues of police brutality and racial profiling by positioning users as witnesses to acts of discrimination, obliging them to make on-the-spot ethical decisions. Similarly, in *Journey through the Camps* (2017–18), he recreates the spaces of the Holocaust, beginning with a grim ride on a crowded prison car destined for Auschwitz. Most impressively of all, in the groundbreaking production, *Haenyeo* (2019), he goes underwater to document the centuries-old, ecologically aware shellfish-diving practices of a small group of women from Jeju Island, South Korea. Following the example of these productions, my goal was – and is – to harness the critical and cognitive capacities of virtual reality in a project centred on Shakespearean drama. Luckily, Jaehee was happy to sign on, and it was at that point that the *Shakespeare-VR* project really began to take shape. Thanks to his reputation and expertise, we were able to borrow a very expensive, state-of-the-art, 3D-360 YI HALO virtual reality camera from Google, thereby alleviating my budget concerns and allowing for a much higher standard of quality than I had originally anticipated.

My other, absolutely essential collaborative relationship was with Sarah Enloe and Ethan McSweeny, Director of Education and Artistic Director (respectively) at the American Shakespeare Center (ASC) in Staunton,

Virginia. Since 2001, the ASC has operated out of the Blackfriars Playhouse, an exquisite, scrupulously crafted recreation of the indoor theatre used by Shakespeare's company. As performers and educators steeped in the fine-grained details of early modern theatrical practice, Sarah and Ethan had a deep interest and intellectual investment in reading Shakespearean drama through the spaces and conditions of original production. When I approached them with the idea of bringing the Blackfriars into virtual reality, they were quick to recognise the educative benefit, but they were also quick to stipulate that any performances we recorded in the theatre would have to take place with the entire theatre fully illuminated, and in front of a live audience (also fully lit). Although these conditions may seem odd to theatregoers accustomed to modern conventions, they are in fact fundamental to the intimate, interactive style of drama that Shakespeare's company produced and are therefore also fundamental to the performance philosophy of the ASC. From my perspective, the stipulations were an entirely welcome advantage, rather than a problem, because a fully lit, fully populated, theatre is an ideal subject for the 360° *mise en scène* made available by virtual reality. It was a natural fit.

So, in November 2018, Jaehee, Ralph, and I brought the 3D-360 YI HALO camera to Staunton, Virginia, for a day of shooting at the ASC. In addition to a four-minute virtual documentary about the Blackfriars stage, we produced virtual productions of four soliloquies from *Hamlet* featuring ASC actor Zoe Speas, who delivered a clever, charismatic performance that contrasted macho nonchalance against bursts of wide-eyed adolescent exuberance. Although we weren't entirely satisfied with the oddly distanced perspective necessitated by the virtual reality camera, Speas' dynamism went a long way towards suggesting the connection between performers and spectators we were hoping to convey. Most notably, in her rendition of the soliloquy in Act Two, Scene Two, she follows the opening line, 'Now I am alone,' with a pause and a smirking glance at the fully lit audience members seated only a few feet away. Tickled by the moment of metatheatrical recognition, her putatively non-existent interlocutors responded with reciprocal smirks and murmurs of amusement. Although authorial intention is always an enigma, my presumption is that Shakespeare anticipated a similar response.

The first official demonstration of our pilot production took place in July 2019 at the 'Digitizing the Stage' conference at Oxford University (www.digitizingthestage.wordpress.com), with curious attendees lining up in the lobby of the Weston Library to try on a VR headset – many for the first time ever. Further demonstrations followed later that year at the Blackfriars conference in Staunton and at various events around Carnegie Mellon. By my best estimation, I have personally shown the project to a thousand people thus far.

In addition to the in-person demonstrations, somewhere near fifteen hundred people have engaged with the *Shakespeare-VR* project online. Pursuant to our goal of maximum accessibility, all project resources – including the virtual media, raw footage, lesson plans, and data from classroom tests – are available at no cost whatsoever through the project website. Moreover, in accordance with the sustainability plan developed by our web designer, Matthew Lincoln, all project resources have a permanent home in CMU's institutional repository, KiltHub, which also serves as the primary access point for users to download the media files for use on their personal VR headsets. To ensure that project resources will be available for the long-term foreseeable future, CMU's Dietrich College of Humanities and Social Sciences has committed to host the content of the project website in perpetuity, with technical support provided by CMU Libraries' research software engineering group. In another effort aimed towards sustainability, our designer used Jekyll to build the site with static (or flat) webpages, thereby escaping the need for a costly database-backed web application and minimising requirements for ongoing maintenance (interested parties may access the source code here: www.github.com/cmu-lib/shakespeare_vr). Although we don't really recommend it, users also have the option to access our virtual reality media through YouTube – a less-than-ideal option because streaming sites tend to reduce picture quality. Ultimately, our intention is to reach as wide as possible audience, and to make project resources available to any instructor, student, or Shakespeare enthusiast anywhere in the world.

With a prototype and a website thus established, I began to turn my attention to the (ongoing) challenge of classroom application. Working in conjunction with a group of pedagogical specialists from CMU's Eberly Center for Teaching Excellence (Jessica Harrell, Soniya Gadgil, and Judith Brooks), and with indispensable assistance from a student in the Human Computer Interaction programme (Thomas Serban von Davier), I developed a lesson plan oriented towards the collection of qualitative and quantitative data (www.shakespeare-vr.library.cmu.edu/curriculum). Because we were working with living human subjects (students in my undergraduate Shakespeare class), we had to submit our plans for the tests to an internal review board in order to ensure compliance with regulatory and conflict of interest issues guidelines – a lengthy process that was entirely new to me (my research typically centres on human subjects who are no longer alive, such as William Shakespeare). In order to measure the impact of the virtual reality media, our testing regimen divided the students into two groups, with each group studying a pair of Shakespearean soliloquies under slightly different pedagogical conditions. In the first group, students studied the soliloquies in formats that included text and two-dimensional video (the 1996 film adaptation of *Hamlet* and a 2014 filmed production of *Hamlet* by the Royal Shakespeare Company). In the second group, students viewed the same performances under the same conditions, but their programme also included the added benefit of the *Shakespeare-VR* virtual reality media. In terms of structure, our assessment plan was very simple: trials for the first group (text + 2D video) provided a benchmark for assessing the effect of the virtual reality intervention in trials for the second group (text + 2D video + VR).

In both trials, students responded to a prompt that probed their ability to (i) identify implicit aspects of spatiality and performance in a dramatic text, (ii) describe how issues of spatiality and performance might impact dramatic effect, and (iii) apply an understanding of these issues to an interpretive assessment. Following the trial, we evaluated the responses according to the following rubric: (i) no impact on targeted learning outcomes, (ii) basic impact on learning outcomes, (ii) advanced impact on learning outcomes. In the final tally, results suggested that that students in the second group (text + 2D video + VR) were more than twice as likely to integrate an awareness of the spatial aspects of performance (such as audience visibility and proximity) into an interpretive assessment. Although these results were encouraging, it is important to note that we were working with a limited sample size,

Figure 2 The 3D-360 YI HALO virtual reality camera at the Blackfriars Playhouse, Blackfriars Playhouse, November 2018

so it would be premature to draw any general conclusions about the efficacy of the virtual reality intervention. On a similar note, I should also point out that, unlike a scientific experiment, the classroom tests did not set out to prove anything one way or another. As is often the case with humanities scholars, I tend to be sceptical about methodologies that purport to quantify learning

Figure 3 Zoe Speas performs the 'poor Yorick' soliloquy. Blackfriars Playhouse, November 2018

outcomes, not only because critical creativity is by its very nature unmeasurable, but also because a focus on data threatens to flatten and trivialise the diverse, complex outcomes that proceed from quality humanities instruction. Irrespective of these reservations, however, my experience with the *Shakespeare-VR* project has helped me to see the tremendous value of classroom tests as a framework for thinking systematically about what one hopes to accomplish, and how. From this perspective, the primary value of the trials inheres, not so much in the hard data they have produced, but in the logistical and pedagogical challenges they have helped to bring into the foreground.

As the *Shakespeare-VR* project moves forward, I hope to make better use of the interactive, medium-specific affordances of virtual reality, and to take up Jennifer Roberts-Smith's challenge to think in terms of what Shakespeare can do for virtual reality, rather than vice versa (see Section 1). When I started the project in 2017, my ambitions centred primarily on documentation and simulation: I simply wanted to offer students a virtual experience of the Shakespearean theatre. Although I still think this basic concept is entirely worthwhile (as far as it goes), my experiences over the past three years have led me to a more nuanced appreciation of virtual reality as an art form in its own right. Thus, in addition to using the medium to think about theatre, I also want to make it think about itself, so to speak, by finding novel ways to build in more subtle opportunities for interactivity, reflexivity, and reflection, and by engaging with it on its own terms as a representative art form that is not especially different from any other representative art form, such as theatre, the novel, or film. On a similar note, I have come to the opinion that, although we are probably stuck with it, the term 'virtual reality' is misleading, or at least unhelpful, because it suggests that the experience one has upon engagement with the medium is somehow an imitative 'virtual' version of something that is putatively more real, or 'actually' real. The truth, however, is much grander. One does not disappear into another reality by looking into an Oculus headset, just as one does not disappear into another reality by turning on a television set or taking a seat at the theatre. Rather, the experience virtual reality makes possible is an extended exercise in imaginative absorption – a very real, profoundly important, aspect of the human condition.

Annotated Bibliography

Justin Carpenter

This annotated bibliography is in two sections, 'Scholarship on VR' and 'Shakespeare VR Projects'.

Scholarship on VR

1. Atkinson, S., and Kennedy, H. W. (2018). Extended Reality Ecosystems: Innovations in Creativity and Collaboration in the Theatrical Arts. *Refractory: A Journal of Entertainment Media*, 30(10). https://refractory-journal.com/30-atkinson-kennedy
   Atkinson and Kennedy discuss the emerging field of extended reality (XR) in the UK, examining four case studies of VR or 360-degree video projects. This article is particularly useful for those who wish to implement XR into their design principles, as it focuses on the role of what the authors refer to as the 'virtual reality production ecosystem'. This ecosystem connects artists with those producing VR experiences, bridging the gap between technical and creative collaborators.

2. Bloom, G., Kemp, S., Toothman, N., and Buswell, E. (2016). 'A Whole Theater of Others': Amateur Acting and Immersive Spectatorship in the Digital Shakespeare Game *Play the Knave*. *Shakespeare Quarterly*, 67(4), 408–30. dx.doi.org/10.1353/shq.2016.0054
   The authors discuss the Shakespeare-based game *Play the Knave*, which they describe as 'a cross between karaoke and machinima'. Observing *Play the Knave* installations leads to two major realisations: first, that over-the-top gestures are easier to capture on camera, and second, that these gestures lead to a crowd forming around the player. This kind of amateur performance and communal gathering couches Shakespeare in a more 'communal, collaborative' experience. This blurs the lines between analogue and digital spaces in a way that avoids the typically agonistic element of games. Instead, it builds a local community of amateur performers through its formal features.

3. Harvey, M., Deuel, A., and Marlatt, R. (2020). 'To Be, or Not to Be': Modernizing Shakespeare with Multimodal Learning Stations. *Journal of Adolescent & Adult Literacy*, 63(5), 559–68. doi:10.1002/jaal.1023

   Harvey, Deuel, and Marlatt survey 100 eighth-grade English language arts (ELA) students and classroom experiments with virtual and augmented reality. They argue for the necessity of multimodal instructional approaches to teaching contemporary adolescents, as these students have been raised in a more multimodal environment. Multimodal fluency informs not only what students want to read or experience, but also how they learn and think. As such, ELA teachers should embrace multimodal approaches for the same reasons that science teachers update their tools: for the sake of better learning and better research methods.

4. Hunter, E. B. (2020). Enactive Spectatorship, Critical Making, and Dramaturgical Analysis: Building *Something Wicked*, the *Macbeth* Video Game. *International Journal of Performance Arts and Digital Media*, 16(1), 1–17. doi:10.1080/14794713.2019.1633830

   This article is a companion essay to *Something Wicked*, a video game adaptation of Shakespeare's *Macbeth*. Hunter argues that the game is a form of critical making that emphasises the process of making as 'a dialogue with a discipline's critical apparatus'. Hunter writes an auto-ethnographic account of how spectator-based revelations about the game's design, along with the iterative design process of critical making, offered insight into how Shakespeare is perceived inside and outside of the humanities, how text and interactive visual experience interact, and how certain design decisions – for example, something as simple as using a Shakespearean work in a violent video game – can prove distracting because games and virtual experiences are difficult to produce and require selectivity with the source material.

5. Merchant, Z., Goetz, E. T., Cifuentes, L., Keeney-Kennicutt, W., and Davis, T. J. (2014). Effectiveness of Virtual Reality-Based Instruction on Students' Learning Outcomes in K-12 and Higher Education: A Meta-analysis. *Computers & Education*, 70, 29–40. doi. org/10.1016/j.compedu.2013.07.033

   The authors perform a meta-analysis of virtual technology-based instruction (games, simulation, virtual worlds) in K-12 or higher education contexts. Of note for VR designers are the results of these pedagogical experiments: first, that games offered higher potential for learning than other virtual technology-based instruction methods and, second, that virtual worlds proved less effective the more they were experienced. This novelty effect could, perhaps, be mitigated by incorporating game-like elements, though the collaborative nature of virtual spaces in the classroom could be a limitation in and of itself.

6. Pietroszek, K., Eckhardt, C., and Tahai, L. (2018). *Hamlet*: Directing Virtual Actors in Computational Live Theater. *Virtual Reality Software and Technology*, ACM (VRST 18), 1–2. doi:10.1145/3281505.3281600

   The authors discuss their virtual reality prototype 'Hamlet', which places players in the role of a theatre director who directs a virtual actor named Adam to perform a famous soliloquy from *Hamlet*. The authors note that theatre and virtual reality share many characteristics – namely, both are immersive while requiring the audience's wilful engagement with the medium as a construction. How theatrical performances or virtual reality worlds engage the audience – who becomes either active or passive – is a by-product of the multisensory qualities of theatrical and virtual reality experiences. 'Hamlet' takes these similarities seriously, fostering an active audience who directs virtual agents in virtual space, thus immersing them in the theatrical world.

7. Rall, H., Reinhuber, E., and Weber, W. (2017). Adapting Shakespeare for Virtual Reality: Defining an Integrated Research Framework. *Proceedings from CONFIA (International Conference on Illustration and Animation)*, 490–500.

   Rall, Reinhuber, and Weber discuss what makes a successful adaptation of Shakespeare, particularly one which uses animation and virtual reality. This narrow focus on animated VR is relevant because animation is a type of film but is distinct from live-action film, as it can be non-representative and therefore unrealistic. This means that animation is more abstract, using formal elements like colour and movement to express internal states of mind. The authors argue that animation's artificiality serves as a proxy for Shakespeare's highly constructed language, suggesting that more abstract representations might better represent his works.

8. Roberts-Smith, J., DeSouza-Coelho, S., and Malone, T. (2016). Staging Shakespeare in Social Games: Towards a Theory of Theatrical Game Design. *Borrowers and Lenders*, 10(1).

   Roberts-Smith, DeSouza-Coelho, and Malone discuss their experiences designing a game-based Shakespeare project, *Staging Shakespeare*. This project was designed to convey the idea of theatricality itself. In this sense, being able to manipulate the stage of a Shakespearean performance communicates to players the ways in which theatrical things and bodies are arranged as means of communicating different ideas. Much like other projects mentioned in this bibliography, the process of designing *Staging Shakespeare* revealed to the authors several key notions about what theatricality is. In particular, theatrical experiences resemble emergent gameplay – authors and readers serve as agents who co-create the unique experience of the text –suggesting that closer attention to the structure of emergence in electronic media could offer some sense of how to better translate Shakespeare into the virtual classroom.

9. Tcha-Tokey, K., Christmann, O., Loup-Escande, E., Loup, G., and Richir, S. (2018). Towards a Model of User Experience in Immersive Virtual Environments. *Advances in Human-Computer Interaction*, 2018, 1–10. doi.org/10.1155/2018/7827286

   The authors of this article attempt to develop a model that accounts for user experience (UX) in immersive virtual environments. To do so, the authors compiled a list of ten key terms that are heavily featured in the literature about virtual environments: *presence, engagement, immersion, flow, usability, skill, emotion, experience consequence, judgement,* and *technology adoption*. A survey performed using these terms was completed by 152 participants. This survey had several hypotheses which shaped the way it was performed: first, that low experience consequence and presence were directly related; second, that presence is increased by engagement and immersion; third, that skill increases a sense of flow, making the experience more usable and emotional; and fourth, that the experience consequence determines the overall efficacy of the VR experience. Many of these suppositions prove true here, at least in part; however, the first hypothesis is incorrect because experience consequence informs flow, which then informs presence. Ultimately, these terms provide a useful model for charting user experience in VR.

10. Ullyot, M. (2018). 'Wear Your Eyes Thus': Toward a Cognitive Ecology of VR Shakespeare. *Shakespeare Association of America Annual Meeting*. dx.doi.org/10.17613/b4bt-2162

In this conference presentation, Ullyot considers Orson Welles' 1951 adaptation of *Othello*, reflecting on the distinctions between film adaptations of Shakespeare and the more immersive quality of VR experiences. Rather than providing a more voyeuristic perspective often seen in film – with the audience left outside of the text looking in through a framed perspective – VR directly implicates the audience to the point where the audience might experience a play directly on the stage. As Ullyot claims, the viewer's perspective 'is fixed, but our orientation toward that action is fluid ... Without a frame, our eyes can wander freely' (3). As a result, VR requires a different attitude towards certain theatrical elements – such as scene transitions and spectator movement – which are fundamentally distinct from more filmic elements where perspective is fixed within the frames of the director's camera-eye.

11. Warren, A. (2018). Virtual Perspective: The Aesthetic Lineages of Immersive Experience. *Refractory: A Journal of Entertainment Media*, 30, 1–16. www.refractory-journal.com/30-warren.

Warren performs a literature review of immersive experiences in historical aesthetics, arguing that VR is part of a long-ranging history of art and immersion. After situating VR in this lineage, Warren contends that the history of the theatre might offer a means of understanding the possible limitations and affordances of VR. Further, the theatre offers a model for discussing key aspects of VR experience, especially immersion. As a result, analyses of the theatre and VR provide both the discursive foundation and critical vantage necessary for reflections on the nature of theatrical design and VR experiences.

Shakespeare VR (AR/XR/MR) Projects

1. *Hamlet 360: Thy Father's Spirit.* (2019). www.commshakes.org/produc
   tion/hamlet-360-thy-fathers-spirit
   Hamlet 360 is a cinematic, 360-degree adaptation of Shakespeare's
   Hamlet which uses VR to place the audience in the play while it is
   performed. The animated quality of VR is used to present the play inside
   of a run-down hall. Throughout the room, Hamlet's memories (featuring objects from other scenes of the play) are visible. This effect blurs
   the lines between the actors – who are real people – and the unrealistic,
   dreamy space which invites the audience to explore it and, thus, discover
   the play through its objects, architecture, and mood.

2. *Play the Knave* (2016). www.playtheknave.org/contact.html
   Play the Knave is a mixed reality video game that allows players to
   manipulate objects and avatars, creating their own personal performance
   of Shakespeare's plays. The game uses Microsoft's Kinect motion-
   sensing camera while presenting on screen the lines of the play for the
   player to read aloud. As a result, the avatar mirrors the detected player
   who performs the lines, making their own Shakespeare short film.

3. *Tempest* (2020). www.//tenderclaws.com/tempest
   Tempest is a VR theatrical experience made by Tender Claws. *Tempest* is
   an animated, dreamlike experience that features one actor and up to
   eight spectators collaborating inside a virtual world. The actor performs
   the role of Prospero, who then casts the audience members as characters
   in the story.

4. Wittek, S. (2020). *Shakespeare VR.* Carnegie Mellon University. doi.
   org/10.1184/R1/c.4704857.v1
   The *Shakespeare-VR* project uses VR technology to bring students into
   direct contact with various Shakespearean soliloquies performed by
   professional actors. It aims to create an open-source tool for teachers
   to teach Shakespeare, even offering lesson plans and worksheets.

5. *Shakespeare XR* (2019). www.shakespeare.org.uk/visit/shakespeares-
   new-place/shakespeare-xr.
   Shakespeare XR is an augmented and virtual reality experience of
   Shakespeare's New Place, his final home. The project overlays the

now demolished house with the live background where it once sat, offering 180-degree perspectives on rooms in the house. A project focused more on cultural heritage and public education, Shakespeare XR is funded by the Arts Council England as part of the Shakespeare Birthplace Trust's creative programme.

References

Aebischer, P., Greenhalgh, S., and Osborne, L. (eds.) (2018). *Shakespeare and the 'Live' Theatre Broadcast Experience*. London: Bloomsbury.

Arora, G., and Milk, C. (2015). *Clouds over Sidra*. Virtual reality film. http://unvr.sdgactioncampaign.org/cloudsoversidra/#.YLjxOS1h1pQ

Badsa, K. (2017). Critique: 'Clouds over Sidra'. *The Migrant & Refugee 'Crisis'*. Emory University. https://scholarblogs.emory.edu/themigrantandrefugeecrisis/2017/11/12/critique-clouds-over-sidra

Bailenson, J. (2018). *Experience on Demand: What Virtual Reality Is, How It Works, and What It Can Do*. New York: W. W. Norton.

Banks, F. (2014). *Creative Shakespeare: The Globe Education Guide to Practical Shakespeare*. London: Bloomsbury Arden Shakespeare.

Baudrillard, J. (1983). *Simulations*. Translated by P. Foss, P. Patton, and P. Beitchman. New York: Semiotext(e).

Baudrillard, J. (1996). *Simulacra and Simulation*. Translated by S. F. Glaser. Ann Arbor: University of Michigan Press.

Best, S., and Marcus, S. (2009). Surface Reading: An Introduction. *Representations*, 108(1), 1–21.

Biocca, F. and Delaney, B. (1995). 'Immersive virtual reality technology. In Communication *In The Age Of Virtual Reality*. Biocca, F. and Levy, M., eds. Hillsdale, N.J.: L. Erlbaum Associates, 57–126.

Biocca, F., Harms, C., and Burgoon, J. K. (2003). Toward a More Robust Theory and Measure of Social Presence: Review and Suggested Criteria. *Presence: Teleoperators and Virtual Environments*, 12(5), 456–80.

Bloom, G. (2018). *Gaming the Stage: Playable Media and the Rise of English Commercial Theater*. Ann Arbor: University of Michigan Press.

Blumstein, G. (16 October 2019). Research: How Virtual Reality Can Help Train Surgeons. *Harvard Business Review*. https://hbr.org/2019/10/research-how-virtual-reality-can-help-train-surgeons

Boenisch, P. M. (2006). Aesthetic Art to Aesthetic Act: Theatre, Media, Intermedial Performance. In C. Kattenbelt and F. Chapple (eds.), *Intermediality in Theatre and Performance*. Amsterdam: Rodopi, 103–16.

Boluk, S., and LeMieux, P. (2017). *Metagaming: Playing, Competing, Spectating, Cheating, Trading, Making, and Breaking Videogames*. Minneapolis: University of Minnesota Press.

Bristol, M. (1996). *Big-Time Shakespeare*. London: Routledge.

Bulu, S. T. (2012). Place, Presence, Social Presence, Co-presence, and Satisfaction in Virtual Worlds. *Computers & Education*, 58(1), 154–61.

Burdick, A. (2012). *Digital Humanities*. Cambridge, MA: MIT Press.

Carey, K. M. (2007). The Aesthetics of Immediacy and Hypermediation: The Dumb Shows in Webster's *The White Devil*. *New Theatre Quarterly*, 23(1), 73–80.

Cauterucci, C. (12 May 2020). I Will Not Be Attending Your Exhausting Zoom Gathering. *Slate*. www.slate.com/human-interest/2020/05/zoom-call-burnout-quarantine.html

Cegys, P. *Blue Hour VR*: Artist Talk on Digital Scenography with Paul Cegys (20 January 2020). Concordia University. www.concordia.ca/cuevents/offices/provost/fourth-space/hosted/2020/01/20/the-blue-hour-vr–artist-talk-on-digital-scenography-with-paul-cegys.html?c=events

Chapple, F., and Kattenbelt, C. (eds.) (2006). *Intermediality in Theatre and Performance*. Rodopi: New York.

Charlton, D. (2012). *Holistic Shakespeare: An Experiential Learning Approach*. Bristol: Intellect.

Cho, Jaehee. Injustice (2015). Virtual reality production.
    Journey through the Camps (2018). Virtual reality production.
    Haenyeo (2019). Virtual reality production.

Clark, A. (2003). *Natural-Born Cyborgs: Minds, Technologies, and the Future of Human Intelligence*. Oxford: Oxford University Press.

Dalgarno, B., and Lee, M. (2010). What Are the Learning Affordances of 3-D Virtual Environments? *British Journal of Educational Technology*, 41 (1), 10–32.

Damer, B., and Hinrichs, R. (2013). The Virtuality and Reality of Avatar Cyberspace. In M. Grimshaw (ed.), *The Oxford Handbook of Virtuality*. Oxford: Oxford University Press, 17–41.

Davenport, T. H., and Beck, J. C. (2001). *The Attention Economy: Understanding the New Currency of Business*. Boston, MA: Harvard Business School Press.

Dawson, A., and Yachnin, P. (2005). *The Culture of Playgoing in Shakespeare's England: A Collaborative Debate*. Cambridge: Cambridge University Press.

Den, F. L. (2011). 'We Confound Knowledge with Knowledge': Posthumanism and Sensory Encounter in John Webster's *The White Devil*. *Cahiers Élisabéthains*, 80(Autumn), 35–46.

Esrock, E. J. (2019). Body Forth in Narrative. In M. Grishakova and M. Poulaki (eds.), *Narrative Complexity*. Lincoln: University of Nebraska Press, 270–90.

Floyd-Wilson, M. (2013). *Occult Knowledge, Science, and Gender on the Shakespearean Stage*. New York: Cambridge University Press.

Fowler, C. (2015). Virtual Reality and Learning: Where Is the Pedagogy? *British Journal of Educational Technology*, 46(2), 412–22.

Freeman, S., Eddy, S. L., McDonough, M., Smith, M. K., Okoroafor, N., Jordt, H., and Wenderoth, M. P. (2014). Active Learning Increases Student Performance in Science, Engineering, and Mathematics. *Proceedings of the National Academy of Sciences*, 111(23), 8410–15.

Gibson, R. (1998). *Teaching Shakespeare*. Cambridge: Cambridge University Press.

Gibson, W. (1984). *Neuromancer*. New York: Ace Books.

Gochfield, D. (dir.) (2017). *To Be with Hamlet*. Created by J. Molina.

Goldberg, D. (1987). 'By Report': The Spectator As Voyeur in Webster's *The White Devil*. *English Literary Renaissance*, 17(Winter), 67–84.

Grau, O. (2003). *Virtual Art: From Illusion to Immersion*. Cambridge, MA: MIT Press.

Grimshaw, M. (2014). *The Oxford Handbook of Virtuality*. Oxford: Oxford University Press.

Groux, C. (21 April 2020). 'Animal Crossing' Inspires Teacher to Help Students Graduate in a Pandemic. *Newsweek*. www.newsweek.com/animal-crossing-new-horizons-teacher-help-students-graduate-pandemic-1498760

Harris, E. A. (25 January 2019). 'Hamlet' in Virtual Reality Casts the Viewer in the Play. *New York Times*. www.nytimes.com/2019/01/25/theater/hamlet-virtual-reality-google.html

Harrison, C. (2016). Are Computers, Smartphones, and the Internet a Boon or a Barrier for the Weaker Reader? *Journal of Adolescent & Adult Literacy*, 60(2), 221–5.

Hayles, K. (2012). *How We Think: Digital Media and Contemporary Technogenesis*. Chicago: University of Chicago Press.

Home, H. (1765). *Elements of Criticism, Vol. I*. London: A. Millar.

Hunter, E. B. (2020). Enactive Spectatorship, Critical Making, and Dramaturgical Analysis: Building *Something Wicked*, the Macbeth Video Game. *International Journal of Performance Arts and Digital Media*, 16(1), 1–7. doi:10.1080/14794713.2019.1633830

ImagineNative 2167 VR tour (2018–19). Virtual reality project commissioned and produced by the Toronto International Film Festival, ImagineNATIVE, PInnguaq, and the Initiative for Indigenous Futures. www.banffcentre.ca/events/imaginenative-2167-tour

Jarvis, L. (2019). *Immersive Embodiment: Theatres of Mislocalized Sensation*. Cham: Palgrave.

Joffe, J. (6 October 2020). Fareed Zakaria Looks at Life after the Pandemic. *New York Times*.

Jurgenson, N. (2012). When Atoms Meet Bits: Social Media, the Mobile Web, and Augmented Revolution. *Future Internet* 4, 83–91. doi:10.3390/fi4010083

Karim-Cooper, F. (2014). Sensing the Past: Tablets and Early Modern Scholarship. In C. Carson and P. Kirwan (eds.), *Shakespeare and the Digital World: Redefining Scholarship and Practice*. New York: Cambridge University Press, 33–42.

Keen, M. (1984). *Chivalry*. New Haven, CT: Yale University Press.

Knoller, N. (2019). Complexity and the Userly Text. In M. Grishakova and M. Poulaki (eds.), *Narrative Complexity*. Lincoln: University of Nebraska Press, 98–120.

Kwon, J., Park, M., Yoon, I., and Park, S. (2012). Effects of Virtual Reality on Upper Extremity Function and Activities of Daily Living Performance in Acute Stroke: A Double-Blind Randomized Clinical Trial. *NeuroRehabilitation*, 31(4), 379–85.

Lagorio, C. (7 January 2007). The Ultimate Distance Learning. *New York Times*. www.nytimes.com/2007/01/07/education/edlife/07innovation.html

Lanier, D. (2010). Recent Shakespeare Adaptation and the Mutations of Cultural Capital. *Shakespeare Studies*, 38, 104–13.

Lanier, J. (2017). *Dawn of the New Everything: Encounters with Reality and Virtual Reality*. New York: Henry Holt.

Lion-Bailey, C., and Lubinsky, J. (2020). *Reality Bytes: Innovative Learning Using Augmented and Virtual Reality*. New York: Dave Burgess Consulting, Inc.

Liu, A. (2013). The Meaning of the Digital Humanities. *PMLA* 128(2), 409–23.

Maler, S. (dir.) (2019). *Hamlet 360: Thy Father's Spirit*. Commonwealth Shakespeare Company and Sensorium

Manarin, K., Carey, M., Rathburn, M., Ryland, G., and Hutchings, P. (2015). Can Students Read? In *Critical Reading in Higher Education: Academic Goals and Social Engagement* eds., Manarin, K., Carey, M.,

Rathburn, M., Ryland, G., and Hutchings, P. Bloomington: Indiana University Press, 2015, 29–46.

Marshall, C. (1993). Wrestling As Play and Game in *As You Like It*. *SEL*, 33 (Spring), 265–87.

McInnis, D. (2013). *Mind-Travelling and Voyage Drama in Early Modern England*. New York: Palgrave Macmillan.

McLuhan, M. (1994). *Understanding Media: The Extensions of Man*. Cambridge, MA: MIT Press.

Merchant, Z., Goetz, E. T., Cifuentes, L., Keeney-Kennicutt, W., and Davis, T. J. (2014). Effectiveness of Virtual Reality-Based Instruction on Students' Learning Outcomes in K-12 and Higher Education: A Meta-analysis. *Computers & Education*, 70, 29–40.

Metz, C. (1975). *The Imaginary Signifier: Psychoanalysis and the Cinema*. Translated by C. Britton, A. Williams, and A. Guzzetti. Bloomington and Indianapolis: Indiana University Press.

Moore, M. G. (1972). Learner Autonomy: The Second Dimension of Independent Learning. *Convergence*, 5(2), 76–88.

Moore, M. G. (1991). Editorial: Distance Education Theory. *American Journal of Distance Education*, 5(3), 1–6.

Murray, J. (2017). Hamlet *on the Holodeck: The Future of Narrative in Cyberspace*. Updated edition. Cambridge, MA: MIT Press.

Nicholson, D. T., Chalk, C., Funnell, W. R. J., and Daniel, S. J. (2006). Can Virtual Reality Improve Anatomy Education? A Randomized Controlled Study of a Computer-Generated Three-Dimensional Anatomical Ear Model. *Medical Education*, 40(11), 1081–7.

Pollard, T. (2005). *Drugs and Theater in Early Modern England*. Oxford: Oxford University Press.

Prince, M. (2004). Does Active Learning Work? A Review of the Research. *Journal of Engineering Education*, 93(3), 223–31.

Proske, L. (2 January 2020). Interviewed by Jennifer A. Low.

Purser, R. (2019). *McMindfulness: How Mindfulness Became the New Capitalist Spirituality*. London: Repeater Books.

Ratto, M. (2011). Critical Making. In *Open Design Now*. B. van Abel, L. Evers, R. Klaassen, and P. Troxler, eds. Amsterdam: BIS.

Richie's Plank Experience VR: THE SCARIEST FUN! (HTC Vive Virtual Reality) (www.youtube.com/watch?v=kGSMypiRsd8).

Ridington. R. (1998). Coyote's Cannon. *American Indian Quarterly*, 22(3), 343–62.

Rokem, F. (2010). *Philosophers and Thespians: Thinking Performance*. Stanford, CA: Stanford University Press.

Rosen, L. D. (2017). The Distracted Student Mind: Enhancing Its Focus and Attention. *The Phi Delta Kappan*, 99(2), 8–14.

Rubin, P. (2018). *Future Presence: How Virtual Reality Is Changing Human Connection, Intimacy, and the Limits of Ordinary Life*. New York: Harper Collins.

Ryan, M. L. (2001). *Narrative As Virtual Reality: Immersion and Interactivity in Literature and Electronic Media*. Baltimore, MD: Johns Hopkins University Press.

Ryle, J., Benesiinaabandan, S., Goulet, D., Chacon, R., Twist, K., and Martínez, C. (2017). Indigenous Existence *Is* Resistance: The Artists of *2167* Discuss Indigenous Futurism, Their Impressions of VR, and Why Canada 150 Isn't the Milestone They're Interested In. www.tiff.net/the-review/indigenous-existence-is-resistance

Salen, K., and Zimmerman, E. (2003). *Rules of Play: Game Design Fundamentals*. Cambridge, MA: MIT Press.

Sampaio, D., & Almeida, P. (2016). Pedagogical Strategies for the Integration of Augmented Reality in ICT Teaching and Learning Processes. *Procedia Computer Science*, 100, 894–9.

Sanchez-Vives, M., and Slater, M. (2005). From Presence to Consciousness through Virtual Reality. *Nature Reviews Neuroscience*, 6, 332–9.

Shakespeare, W. (1995). *Henry V*. Edited by T. W. Craik. London: Bloomsbury.

Shakespeare, W. (2017). *A Midsummer Night's Dream*. Edited by S. Chaudhuri. London: Bloomsbury.

Shakespeare, W. (2012). *Romeo and Juliet*. Edited by R. Weis. London: Bloomsbury.

Shakespeare, W. (2013). *The Winter's Tale*. Edited by J. Pitcher. London: Bloomsbury.

Shellard, D., and Keenan, S. (2016). *Shakespeare's Cultural Capital*. London: Palgrave Macmillan UK.

Sherman, N. (2 June 2020). Zoom Sees Sales Boom amid Pandemic. *BBC News*. www.bbc.co.uk/news/business-52884782

Sidney, P. (1970). *An Apology for Poetry*. Edited by F. G. Robinson. New York: Macmillan.

Simon, R. (2011). Afterword: The Turn to Pedagogy: A Needed Conversation on the Practice of Curating Difficult Knowledge. In E. Lehrer, C. Milton, and M. Patterson (eds.), *Curating Difficult Knowledge: Violent Pasts in Public Places*. New York: Palgrave Macmillan, 193–209.

Sobchack, V. (1995). Phenomenology and the Film Experience. In L. Williams (ed.), *Viewing Positions: Ways of Seeing Film*. New Brunswick, NJ: Rutgers University Press, 36–58.

Spaull, S. (24 July 2019). Four Reasons VR Gaming Still Isn't Mainstream. *Minutehack*. www.minutehack.com/opinions/four-reasons-vr-gaming-still-isnt-mainstream

Spellberg, M. (2013). Feeling Dreams in *Romeo and Juliet*. *English Literary Renaissance*, 43(1), 62–85.

Tribble, E., and Sutton, J. (2011). Cognitive Ecology As a Framework for Shakespearean Studies. *Shakespeare Studies*, 39, 94–103.

UK's Internet Use Surges to New Highs during Lockdown (24 June 2020). *BBC News*. www.bbc.co.uk/news/technology-53149268

Wallace, J., and Patrick, V. (27 April 2020). Life in Lockdown Is Testing Parents' Bandwidth, but There Are Ways to Protect Your Mental Energy. *Washington Post*. www.washingtonpost.com/lifestyle/2020/04/27/life-lockdown-is-testing-parents-bandwidth-heres-how-protect-your-mental-energy

Warwick, C., Terras, M., and Nyhan, J., eds. (2012). *Digital Humanities in Practice*. London: Facet.

Waterworth, J. A., and Waterworth. E. L. (2014). Distributed Embodiment: Real Presence in Virtual Bodies. In Mark Grimshaw (ed.), *The Oxford Handbook of Virtuality*. Oxford: Oxford University Press, 589–601.

Webster, J. (1972). *The White Devil*. In D. C. Gunby (ed.), *Three Plays*. Reprint, London: Penguin, 1995, 33–166.

Weech, S., Kenny, S., and Barnett-Cowan., M. (2019). Presence and Cybersickness in Virtual Reality Are Negatively Related: A Review. *Frontiers in Psychology*, vol. 10, article 158. doi.org/10.3389/fpsyg.2019.00158

White, R. S. (2016). *Shakespeare's Cinema of Love: A Study in Genre and Influence*. Manchester: Manchester University Press. Reprint 2020

Wilson, H. R. (2020). New Ways of Seeing, Feeling, Being: Intimate Encounters in Virtual Reality Performance. *International Journal of Performance Arts and Digital Media* 16(2), 114–33.

Worthen, W. B. (2011). Intoxicating Rhythms: Or, Shakespeare, Literary Drama, and Performance (Studies). *Shakespeare Quarterly* 62(3), 303–39.

Worthen, W. B. (2012). 'The Written Troubles of the Brain': *Sleep No More* and the Space of Character. *Theatre Journal*, 64(1), 79–97.

Acknowledgements

The editors wish to thank the series editors, Gillian Woods and Liam Semler, and Emily Hockley at Cambridge University Press for guidance and encouragement as we brought this Element together. Many thanks also to Lindsay Glick for indispensable editorial assistance, and to our families for their love, comfort, and support. This collection started life as a seminar led by the editors at the Shakespeare Association of America's annual meeting in 2020, and we thank the SAA for their support. Funding for this project was made available by the Department of English at Carnegie Mellon University.

Cambridge Elements ≡

Elements in Shakespeare and Pedagogy

Liam E. Semler
University of Sydney

Liam E. Semler is Professor of Early Modern Literature in the
Department of English at the University of Sydney. He is
author of *Teaching Shakespeare and Marlowe: Learning versus
the System* (2013) and co-editor (with Kate Flaherty and Penny
Gay) of *Teaching Shakespeare beyond the Centre: Australasian
Perspectives* (2013). He is editor of *Coriolanus: A Critical Reader*
(2021) and co-editor (with Claire Hansen and Jackie Manuel)
of *Reimagining Shakespeare Education: Teaching and Learning
through Collaboration* (Cambridge, forthcoming). His most
recent book outside Shakespeare studies is *The Early Modern
Grotesque: English Sources and Documents 1500–1700* (2019).
Liam leads the Better Strangers project which hosts the
open-access Shakespeare Reloaded website
(shakespearereloaded.edu.au).

Gillian Woods
Birkbeck College, University of London

Gillian Woods is Reader in Renaissance Literature and Theatre
at Birkbeck College, University of London. She is the author of
Shakespeare's Unreformed Fictions (2013; joint winner of
Shakespeare's Globe Book Award), *Romeo and Juliet: A
Reader's Guide to Essential Criticism* (2012), and numerous
articles about Renaissance drama. She is the co-editor (with

Sarah Dustagheer) of *Stage Directions and Shakespearean Theatre* (2018). She is currently working on a new edition of *A Midsummer Night's Dream* for Cambridge University Press, as well as a Leverhulme-funded monograph about Renaissance Theatricalities. As founding director of the Shakespeare Teachers' Conversations, she runs a seminar series that brings together university academics, school teachers and educationalists from non-traditional sectors, and she regularly runs workshops for schools.

ABOUT THE SERIES

The teaching and learning of Shakespeare around the world is complex and changing. *Elements in Shakespeare and Pedagogy* synthesises theory and practice, including provocative, original pieces of research, as well as dynamic, practical engagements with learning contexts.

Cambridge Elements ☰

Elements in Shakespeare and Pedagogy